-ISTS, -ERS, and -IANS

POTTY LOO BOOK

of

Poems, Jokes, Comments, Ideas, and Observations

To Frank, with thanks for
some great tabletennis on
Arcadia 2017.

Adrian

The author in drag. (Churcher's College 1953)

The author (left) in civvies, jointly receiving the Institution of Electrical Engineers' "J. J. Thompson Award". (Now the Institution of Engineering and Technology)

-ISTS, -ERS, and -IANS

POTTY LOO BOOK

of

Poems, Jokes, Comments, Ideas, and Observations

Adrian F. Fray

First published in the United Kingdom in 2010 by Adrian Forrest Fray, Malvern, Worcestershire.

ISBN 978-0-9538869-2-0 (b&w version ISBN 978-0-9538869-3-7)

Printed by Aspect Design
89 Newtown Road, Malvern, Worcs. WR14 1PD
United Kingdom
Tel: 01684 561567
E-mail: books@aspect-design.net
Website: www.aspect-design.net

Preface

It is my intention that this book should be amusing, informative, controversial, and thought-provoking, with something in it for everyone regardless of age, literacy, or technical ability. If your profession ends with -ist, -er, or -ian, you ought to find something of interest. No one from toilet cleaner to Prime Minister, should feel embarrassed if caught with this book in their possession.

Most of the poems have been written for the amusement of my friends, relatives, or the various clubs and societies of which I am a member. Consequently the book is something of a personal Odyssey, and some poems contain words or statements that require a dedicated introduction. The booklet also includes jokes, comments, observations, and ideas that may provide food for thought. I think you will find it quite different from any other book that you have read. You won't know whether that is a good thing or a bad thing until you have finished it, because you will discover that the style and content change as you progress through it.

You can read short extracts whilst standing on a commuter train, while awaiting a charter flight, an executive jet, a rocket into space, or while simply sitting on the loo. For a longer read, and a bit of interaction, you can use my introduction to analyse my poems and the poems of other poets. You can also criticise my grammar by observing that I like to frequently split infinitives, and may sometimes use a preposition to end a sentence with. (Can you find more than 10 typing, spelling, or grammatical errors?) You may wonder whether the study of English Grammar, the construction of sentences, and the difference between poetry and prose, has slipped off the National Curriculum. Indeed, I know a Professor of English who seems to be unaware of the difference between Poetry and Prose!

In addition to poems, many of the other items will provoke discussion, criticism, or acclaim, from a range of magazines, periodicals, and journals. It should cause some raised eye-brows from readers of the more prestigious journals to find the reference is given as:-

Fray, Adrian F. ; " -ists, -ers, and -ians Potty Loo Book".

In these austere times a little lunacy may brighten their day. To be even more "potty", I have published a Patricians edition in colour, and a Plebeians edition in black and white, with different ISBN numbers for each. It will be interesting to note which ISBN number is quoted. I sincerely hope that you have been able to afford the colour edition.

Contents

*First published in "Mites and Tites"; ISBN 0-9538869-1-3; ©2007.

Introduction

(Primarily for Academic -ians)

Many more than 50 years have passed since I was taught to write poetry, and I have noticed in recent years that there have been many "poetry" books published that show the authors do not appreciate the difference between "poetry" and "prose". I do not want to denigrate prose as it is frequently more beautiful than a poem. This is a consequence of **the restrictive rules that define a poem**. "Art", on the other hand, does not have any defining rules, and it is permissible to describe a pile of bricks, or half a pickled sheep as "Art". This is **NOT** the case for poetry.

- A poem is a metred composition.
- Prose is a non-metred composition.

During the late 19th and early 20th centuries the word 'poetry' began to be used in a different context. A ballet might be described as "poetry in motion", and a really moving piece of prose might be described as "sheer poetry". This usage seems to have led to additional definitions of the word 'poetry' being introduced into dictionaries. When you read this modified definition it gives the impression that ANY verbal composition may be called a poem. That is **EMPHATICALLY NOT TRUE**, and it is surely not what was intended by the modified definition. The word 'poem' **MUST** be allowed to retain its original definition because it is the concept of metre that distinguishes it from prose. That is the sole *raison d'etre* for the term 'poem'. If you dispute this definition you will be implying that the associated definitions, such as iambus, trochee, dactyl, anapaest and amphibrach, are pointless and of no consequence.

There have been many examples of pieces of prose winning competitions that are specifically advertised as "Poetry" competitions, thereby breaking the "Trades Description Act"! Poetry can be clearly defined as having a rhythmical format termed the **"metre"**, whereas prose does not retain a metre. The rhythmic format of a metred composition, is characterized by a **regular** arrangement of stressed and unstressed, or of long and short syllables. These arrangements are like the bars in music, and are termed metrical feet. There are names for seven different metrical feet, and if I use a [u] and a [-] to represent unstressed (de) and stressed (dah) syllables, respectively, then the names and stress are defined as:-

Iambus	| u - |	iambic foot
Trochee	| - u |	trochaic foot

1

Dactyl	| - u u |	dactylic foot
Anapaest	| u u - |	anapaestic foot
Amphibrach	| u - u |	amphibrachic foot
Spondee	| - - |	spondaic foot
Tribrach	| u u u |	tribrachic foot

Greek verses frequently use metric feet containing various arrangements of four syllables, but they have been excluded from the list. The spondee and tribrach occur in some of the classical Latin poems, but poetry in the English language always has one stressed and either one or two unstressed syllable in each metrical foot, and therefore it is only the first five from this list that should be applicable. However, I suppose one could write something like:-

$$\| u - \| u - \| - - \|$$

> I love to go, go, go,
> To play in snow, snow, snow.

When putting poetry to music the main stress is on the first beat of a bar and therefore it may be more convenient to ignore the metrical layout and write the above 'line' as

| *rest* **u** | - **u** | - *rest or hold for bar* | - *rest or hold for bar* | - *rest or hold for bar* |
| *rest* **I** | **love** to **go** | **go** | **go** | |

Sometimes, to force a longer pause between lines, the metrical foot at the end of a line is incomplete. This is known as a "**catalectic**".

A line of a poem is called a "verse", and a group of lines whose metre and rhyming sequence is regularly repeated is called a "stanza", but the term verse is incorrectly used nowadays instead of stanza. A verse, or line of poetry may contain two to eight metrical feet, and these are known as:-

Dimetre	2 metrical feet
Trimetre	3 metrical feet
Tetrametre.........................	4 metrical feet
Pentametre.........................	5 metrical feet
Hexametre (or Alexandrine).....	6 metrical feet
Septametre........................	7 metrical feet
Octametre..........................	8 metrical feet

In general, humorous poems, and some sad ones, are best written with short lines, as anything longer than a pentametre can become rather tedious to read, and is best restricted to epic poems. By way of example consider a stanza from *Faithless Nelly Gray*, by Thomas Hood:-

$$| u - | u - | u - | u - |$$
$$| u - | u - | u - |$$
$$| u - | u - | u - | u - |$$
$$| u - | u - | u - |$$

Ben **Battle was** a **soldier bold**,
And **used** to **war's** al**arms**,
<u>But a</u> **cannon-ball** took **off** his **legs**,
So **he** laid **down** his **arms**!

As you can see, this humorous stanza is a mixture of alternate iambic tetrametres and iambic trimetres. The two words that are underlined have to be pronounced quickly as a single unstressed syllable in order to maintain the metre. This inconsistency can make a poem difficult to read first time round, but may be acceptable, and can even add some zip to humorous verses, once it is noted. This 4-verse (line) stanza only has a single rhyme between the second and forth verses (lines), and is much easier to compose than a stanza with multiple rhymes involving every verse (line). Although this stanza could have been typed as two verses of iambic septametres, the humorous content, and the phrasing (in this case isolated by commas), suggest that the verses should be arranged as tetrametres and trimetres.

Poetry doesn't have to be written in stanzas, nor does it have to include rhymes. Provided that it has metre, it may be called a poem. The poem, *Hiawatha*, by Henry Wadsworth Longfellow, does not have regular stanzas or rhymes, but it definitely IS a poem. Consider the verses:-

$$| - u | - u | - u | - u |$$

By the **shores** of **Git**che **Gu**mee,
By the **shin**ing **Big-Sea-Wa**ter,
Stood the **wig**wam of No**ko**mis,
Daughter **of** the **Moon**, No**ko**mis.
Dark be**hind** it **rose** the **for**est,
Rose the **black** and **gloo**my **pine**-trees,
Rose the **firs** and **cones** up**on** them;
Bright be**fore** it **beat** the **wa**ter,
Beat the **clear** and **sun**ny **wa**ter,
Beat the **shin**ing **Big**-Sea **wa**ter.

These are all trochaic tetrametres with no rhyme, but the rhythm is very apparent. In fact, the trochaic foot, with its emphasis on the first syllable, makes the whole poem glow with energy. (If you read the complete poem you will discover some sections in which Longfellow has clearly encountered difficulty in maintaining the metre.)

Contrast that with these verses of anapaestic tetrametres from *Destruction of Sennacherib*, by Lord George Byron:-

u u -	u u -	u u -	u u -
u u -	u u -	u u -	u u -
u u -	u u -	u u -	u u -
u u -	u u -	u u -	u u -

The Assyrian came **down** like the **wolf** on the **fold**,
And his **co**horts were **gleam**ing in **pur**ple and **gold**;
And the **sheen** of their **spears** was like **stars** on the **sea**,
When the **blue** wave rolls **night**ly on **deep** Galilee.

Although there is no mention of horses or chariots, the **anapaestic foot**, particularly when arranged as tetrametres, immediately gives the impression of galloping horses. Instead of galloping horses, one could use a mixed metre verse to give the impression of a canter or rising-trot.

| u u - | u - | u u - | u - |
| u u - | u - | u u - | u - | etc

'Though the **Prince** looks **great** on an **ungulate**,
At a **Polo** Match or **Affairs** of **State**,
He's a **sister Ann** who's no '**also ran**'.
She's been **winning more** than her **coll**eagues **can**.
When she **jumps** a **fence** she will **seldom fall**,
As she **learnt** her **jump**ing over **Mum's** back **wall**.

These are both examples of '**onomatopæia**', but there are other ways by which a scene may be set. My poetry class was asked to read the first stanza from "The Lady of Shallot" by Alfred, Lord Tennyson, and prepare to answer some questions about it.

On **either side** the **river lie**
Long **fields** of **barley and** of **rye**
That **cloth** the **wold** and **meet** the **sky**.
And **through** the **field** the **road** runs **by**
To **many-tow**ered **Camelot**." etc..

I made a note of the metre and the rhyming sequence, but the first question we were asked was "What was the weather like?" The whole class unanimously agreed that it was a warm sunny day in late summer, yet the poem made no mention of the weather conditions or the time of year!

Single syllable nouns are most likely to require stress, such as 'house' and 'hill' in:-

"The **house** was **built** upon a **hill**."

| u   - | u   - | u - | u - |

However, it can sometimes be more evocative to move the stress away from the noun, as in

"**Our** house is **big**ger than **your** house is !"

| -   u   u | - u   u | -   u   u |

There is then the problem of maintaining that format throughout the poem.

I mentioned that prose can often be more beautiful than poetry due to the restrictions that are imposed upon poetry. The word '**beautiful**' is a good example of what I mean. This word contains three syllables, and during the course of normal speech the first syllable is stressed and the following two are unstressed, as in

| - u u | - u u | - u u | -   (catalectic)

"**Beau**tiful **dream**er, come **hark** unto **me**"

or

| u - u | u - u | u -   (catalectic)

"The **beau**tiful Annabel **Lee**"

Consequently, you would not expect to be able to include this word if you are writing verses using iambic or trochaic metre. If the essence of a poem would be lost without that particular adjective, and you do not want to undertake the task of re-writing the poem in a different format, there are subtle ways in which you can force the third syllable to have a **slight** stress. You can either place it at the end of your iambic verse:-

$$|u-|u-|u-|u-|u-|u-|$$

Although less **bright**, the **sallow moon** is **beautiful**.

Or, place an unstressed syllable followed by a stressed syllable immediately after it;

$$|u-|u-|u-|u-|u-|u-|u-|u-|$$

How **beau**tiful the **sallow moon** that **peers** at **me** through **wispy clouds.**

Some words, particularly conjunctions and prepositions, are not often stressed in normal speech, but may be in poetry. It will become evident whether they are used in a stressed or unstressed location once you have grasped the metre of a poem. You will notice a considerable difference in "poetical quality" as you progress through this book, so don't give up after reading the first three or four poems!

Bearing these aspects in mind, I hope that my humorous, lewd, or personal poems, together with the comments, observations, ideas, and jokes, will provide amusement, pleasure, and food for thought.

6

The Horticulturalists

As this collection of poems, jokes, illustrations, and profound statements has been titled "**-ists, -ers, and -ians Potty Loo Book**", I think it appropriate to begin with four poems, and some profound statements, that are substantially about loos, drains, or slopping out. Some readers may not like one or two of these as they are intended to shock!

This first poem, entitled "The Horticulturalists", is rather like "Ten Green Bottles Hanging on a Wall", but describes three blonde maidens starting life at an Agricultural College in Worcestershire.

The Horticulturalists

```
| u - | u - | u - | u - |
| u - | u - | u - | u - |
| u - | u - | u - | u - |
| u - | u - | u - | u - |
```

Upon the Pershore College lists
Of student Horticulturalists
About to start their 1st degrees,
Were Kath'rine, Susan, and Louise,

But in their Starter Year they found
That double-digging heavy ground,
Or spreading compost on the soil,
Was nothing more than irksome toil.

So Katherine, to help her bring
Some light relief, began to sing,
And that invoked her friends to say
"Your voice gets better, every day."

She practiced with the birds at dawn,
And in the evening on the lawn.
She practiced in the orchard too,
And even practiced on the Loo.

Whilst double-digging, Kitt had found
Her voice acquired an earthy sound,
And Students said, "You should go far.
You have the makings of a star."

And so she left within a year
To settle in a new career,
And for a name that seemed to fit,
The Students called her "Earthy Kitt".

But Susan and Louise went back
To College, where they learnt the knack
Of sowing beds with flower seeds,
And sorting out the flowers from weeds.

This **task** appealed, and **Susan found**
Her **feet** would seldom **touch** the **ground**!
Into the **potting shed** she'd **sneak**,
And **sow** there, **several times a week**.

Just **sowing seeds** gave **Sue** delight.
She **even sowed** them **in the night**
Until she **had** to **leave** and **wed**,
When **seeds** were **sown** within her **bed**.

Her **actions caused** a **great** to-**do**,
And **Students called** her "Seedy **Sue**".
This **isn't how** my **story ends** ......
Louise returned without her **friends**.

Her **final year** was **quickly gone**.
A **lot** of **it** was "**potting-on**",
Or **taking cuttings from** the **trees**.
This **simple task** seduced Louise.

She **potted-on** in **pots** of **blue**,
In **pots** of **red**, and orange **too**;
In **pots** of **wood** and **pots** of **tin**,
Or **wire pots** with **liners in**.

In **huge** great **pots** and **pots** quite **small**;
In **shallow pots** and **pots** quite **tall**;
In **baths**, and **sinks**, and **pudding bowls**
Or **chamber pots** with **drain**age **holes**.

By **now** you **ought** to **know** I **tease**,
And **real**ize **what** they **named** Louise.
If **not**, I **will** enligh**ten you**!
The **Students called** her "**Potty-Lou**"!

The poem is entirely fictitious, and was written after I had decided upon a title for the booklet. I don't know, and never have known, anyone at Pershore College named Katherine, Susan, or Louise, but I am sure that students with these names must have passed through its' portals. If they become subjected to teasing as a result of the poem I offer them my apologies, but they can take some consolation from the fact that their names are in verse.

9

The Privy-Chamber

Private apartments in a royal residence were called "The Privy Chambers", and following from that, a household toilet was nicknamed "The Privy". The word "privy" may originally have been an adjective with a meaning somewhat similar to "private", "clandestine" or "secret", and may subsequently have taken on verbal properties when it became used in phrases such as "to be privy to a secret". This is rather like saying "to be secretly informed of a secret"

Have you ever wondered how we managed before the introduction of toilet paper, particularly in winter when dock leaves might be covered with snow? The Romans built municipal, multi-hole toilets, with a channel of water for washing a sponge. The Normans built toilets in a corner of the bedchambers in their castles. These doubled up as wardrobes because the smell of ammonia kept moths away. Consequently they became known as a "garderobes". The outlet from a garderobe usually dropped straight into the moat, which probably began to smell rather unsavoury after a few months. It is therefore not surprising that nobles would acquire several properties, and peregrinate between them when the odour made it necessary. I have been told that the nobles in these castles would have used a goose's neck instead of a sponge, but royalty could use a swan's neck. When I was about 9 years old, my local vicar, the Rev. Ivor Machin, told me that monks used a roughened stick which was swilled out in a bucket of water, and then hung up for the next monk. Supposedly, this is the origin of the expression "To get hold of the wrong end of the stick!" During the Second World War, when I was a little boy, toilet paper was scarce and expensive. Sheets of newspaper were frequently used as a substitute, and some people preferred the soft texture of newspaper rather than the tracing-paper qualities of Izal or Bronco toilet rolls. Indeed, I frequently used these toilet rolls for tracing. It was many years before toilet rolls received "a puppy-dog" test.

Many poor or slum houses had the privy at the bottom of the garden, and the effluent either drained into a septic tank, or had to be buried in a pit. Richer houses had a "Chamber Pot" which might have been hidden in a piece of furniture or under the bed. During the Victorian era the drainage systems were improved and interior toilets began to be installed in the large houses. One of the manufacturers of toilets and drainage systems was Thomas P. Crapper. He was baptized on the 28th September 1836 and died during January 1910 (probably on the 27th). It is he who is accredited with having developed the "Ball-cock". This was used to control the maximum level that water could reach when flowing into a tank (cistern). It is comprised of a float (usually a ball) on a long arm which is pivoted near the end furthest from the float. As water enters the tank (or cistern), the float (or ball) rises, and the arm closes a rubber valve over the filling orifice (or cock). By pulling a chain (or pressing a button), water is rapidly siphoned out of the cistern to flush the toilet pan. The water can now flow through the cock because the float has dropped, but the flow is kept relatively slow, so the siphon is broken by air leaking in. Consequently the flush stops but water continues to flow into the cistern until the ball is raised high enough to re-close the cock.

The filter beds at Malvern Sewage Works.

This next poem pulls no punches when describing a Privy. It is intended to shock!

The Privy-Chamber

While sitting here upon the throne,
With door that's locked, and all alone,
Consider what you're sitting on,
And what comes in, and what has gone.
Consider how your life would be
Without this flushing lavat'ry,
And do you ever have the fear
Of finding there's no paper here?
If wafted to some distant land
That's waterless with desert sand,
No dock leaves there, or blades of grass,
Consider how you'd wipe your hand!
Or maybe in some different dream
You're in a land where there's a stream,
But sanitation … there is none!
This stream is used by everyone
For washing clothes, and drinking too,
And then they use it as a loo.
It's fairly plain for all to see
The reason why there's dysent'ry.
But here within your privy walls,
Where you can run when nature calls,
Your cistern's loaded to the brink
With water fit enough to drink,
And when it filled, 'twas Crapper's ball
That shut the cock to hold it all.
So when you play your Royal Flush
Your faeces exit with a rush
To pass along your local drain
And join the water sewage main.
They reach a tank for sediments
To settle out impediments
Allowing fluid to be led
Aerated to a filter bed.
From thence it's pumped to river banks,
And that is why you should give thanks
For sewage works by Severn-Trent.
When loos are flushed they're heaven sent
As down the stream you'll find, I think,
The water's pumped back out to drink!

So, by the time it's reached your door
It may have passed through three or four!
Remember now those foreign lands;
Polluted streams and soiled hands.
Don't question what you ought to do,
Just go and buy an OXFAM loo.
Or if you're feeling really swell,
Help OXFAM dig a village well.

Your gift is a lovely loo

OxfamUnwrapped.com

The Cabbage Grower's Lament

I believe I wrote "The Cabbage-Grower's Lament" in 1958 or 1959, and it was the first poem I read at the Hereford Caving Club annual dinner. In those days every member was expected to contribute towards the entertainment in some way. A group might get together to sing or chant a lewd song. Someone might tell jokes or get other members doing silly things. It seems very tame now, but we even played Musical Chairs and Pass-the-Parcel. We made the Musical Chairs more interesting by getting the females to sit on the male laps, and Pass-the-Parcel usually contained some interesting challenges by way of forfeits! I had intended performing a few conjuring tricks as my contribution and I was absent-mindedly thinking of these while walking back to my lodgings one dark night when I nearly fell into a drain whose cover had been removed. I was carrying my caving lamp at the time and so the association of ideas was born.

The photo is of an HCC 'dig' at the Twrch Resurgence, in South Wales. This 'dig' was started about 10 years after I wrote the poem, but it seems an appropriate illustration. We never entered a cave ... in fact we didn't even find a trace of passage, but we got plenty of exercise! I suspect that the water is emerging from a bedding-plane rather than a passage, but the quantity of water flowing out suggests that there ought to be a sizable passage somewhere beneath. If there is a passage, the entrance may be covered by a huge amount of glacial debris left over from the last Ice Age.

The poem was intended to be read to an audience of drunken cavers, and is technically rather poor. There are several 2-syllable words (underlined) that have to be read as a single syllable, and it includes the word "furiously", which some people might try to pronounce as a 4-syllable word. However, if you use my " u & - " terminology to analyze other poet's poems you will find that many of the greatest poems are technically lacking. So don't despair when you try writing your own.

"A Sergeant Major who had been a right "pain-in-the-arse" to his recruits was about to retire from the army. Needless to say, the whole of the barracks were united in giving him an appropriate send-off. He was persuaded that it was a requirement for him to have a full medical check-up before retirement, and to that end he was taken to see the newly qualified MO. The MO put a thermometer in his mouth, took his pulse, and listened to his heart. When he took the thermometer out of Sergeant Major Smithers's mouth, he gave a "Tut tut". He said that, as the thermometer wasn't registering properly, he would have to take the temperature *ad rectum*. Sergeant Major Smithers was therefore required to strip naked and lay face down on the bed while the thermometer was pushed in. As it would take a minute or two, the MO left the room to attend to some paper-work. While he was away the Brigadier came in to say farewell, but his jaw dropped when he saw the naked Smithers.

"Smithers, what the B....y H...l do you think you are doing?"

"I'm having my temperature taken, sir." Smithers replied, twisting his head round slightly.

"Good God man, whoever's heard of anyone having their temperature taken with a daffodil?"

15

The Cabbage Grower's Lament

u -	u -	u -	u -
u -	u -	u -
u -	u -	u -	u -
u -	u -	u -

The **limestone in** our **cabbage patch**
  Con**tained** a **little hole;**
Sur**rounded by** a **wire fence,**
  It **couldn't harm** a **soul.**

But **then** some **ardent** <u>**cavers**</u>
  Came **there** one **day** to **dig,**
And **now** we **can't** grow **cabbages;**
  The **hole's** so **blooming big.**

They **spent** all **day** be**neath** the **earth,**
  And **fur**<u>iou</u>sly they **dug,**
'Till **in** the **evening out** they **popped,**
  Like **glow**-worms **robed in mud.**

Our **dog** be**gan** to **dig** there **too.**
  I**magine his** sur**prise,**
They **were** not **digging for** a **bone,**
  Just **getting exercise.**

Re**porters came** to **see** the **hole.**
  It **got into the** <u>**papers**</u>,
And **people eating fish** and **chips**
  Read **all about** their <u>**capers.**</u>

The **cavers said** they **thought** it "**went**".
  I **said** I **wished** it **had,**
For **digging up** our **cabbage patch**
  Was **making me** grow **mad.**

I **wasn't mad** with **rage** for **long,**
  For **just** a **few** days <u>**after,**</u>
I **ceased** to **curse** and **swear** and **groan,**
  And **nearly died** of <u>**laughter.**</u>

You **should** have **seen** their **looks** of **scorn**,
Dejection **and** dis**dain**,
On **finding that** it **didn't "go"**,
But **joined** a Sew**age Main**!

I am reminded of the three engineering students from Brunel University, Nottingham University, and Southampton University who were gathered at the bar after a Conference. They began discussing who might have designed the human body. The one from Brunel University said, "It must have been a Mechanical Engineer. Just look at the well-articulated joints, and note that they are self-lubricating."

"No, it was definitely an Electrical Engineer", said the student from Nottingham University. The nervous system and brain are so complex, with many thousands of electrical connections.
It has got to be an Electrical Engineer."

The Southampton University student settled the argument. "We can be absolutely certain that it was a Council Engineer", he said. "Who else would run a toxic waste pipeline through a recreational area?"

The Bunkhouse Warden

People involved in outdoor activities such as Climb**ers**, Cav**ers**, Camp**ers**, Archaeolog**ists**, Road-repair**ers**, Construction-work**ers**, and Scout-Mast**ers**, may rent or own a house, cottage, barn, shed, portable-cabin, or tent, for overnight accommodation and/or toilet facilities. If there are several people using the accommodation they will probably elect or employ someone to keep it tidy. Accommodation such as this frequently lacks a flush toilet because there is NO sewage main. Consequently it may be necessary to regularly empty an Elsan. One year it was my turn to be Cottage Warden for the Hereford Caving Club. I noted that the Cottage Warden seemed to get the blame for everything, and that the smallest room contained the greatest wealth of pictures and literature. One day someone wrote on the wall:-

> "This bloody latrine is no use at all.
> The seat is too high and the hole is too small."

and another wit had added:-

> "To this I reply with the obvious retort.
> Your arse is too large and your legs are too short!"

It was probably some of the younger members who were responsible for this vandalism, because writing on walls seems to be a form of occupational therapy for students.

After I became Cottage Warden I discovered that it could be difficult to locate somewhere to empty the Elsan. Not only was the local soil shallow and full of large rocks in the wilds of Wales, but there was also the possibility of finding that someone else had emptied it exactly where I began to dig! I just had to let off steam by writing a crude poem about the Cottage Warden. It was a very inferior poem with poor metre, and no merit, except when read to a drunken audience with personal recollections of the environment described. In order to include it in this Anthology it has been slightly modified, but it is still crude. You could alter it for your own purposes … Scouts, Mountaineers, Builders, etc..

The contents of "-ists, -ers, and -ians Potty Loo Book" will improve!

The Bunkhouse Warden

| u - | u - | u - | u
| u - | u - | u - |
| u - | u - | u - | u
| u - | u - | u - |

I thought as Bunkhouse Warden
  I'd have a cushy job,
Collecting up the lolly,
  From each departing mob,

But found it isn't easy,
  To please all those who come.
Some say they're cared for better,
  When they're at home with Mum!

They've used a pan for frying,
  Already full of fat,
(A trifle stale and rancid
  But none the worse for that),

And never thanked their Warden,
  But said that I'm to blame,
As bacon fried in mildew,
  Just doesn't taste the same!

They said their soup was gritty.
  I had no ill intent;
I'd quite forgot the saucepan
  Was used to mix cement!

And if a little "Rodine",
  Adds flavour to the stew,
They're sure to say the Warden
  Has tried to poison you.

The servile Bunkhouse Warden
  Has got some lousy jobs,
Like clearing up the debris
  Behind departing mobs.

When **asked** if **they'd** be **ti**dy
And **watch** their **Ps** and **Qs**.
They **said**, "It's **up** to **you** mate
To **watch** our **Pees** and **Poohs**,

The **torn**-up "**Daily Mi**rrors"
Have **got** to **be** re**placed**,
And **all** that **crass** graffiti
Will **have** to **be** ef**faced**.

The "**Elsan**" **must** be **empt**ied
(There's **not** a **sew**age **main**).
I'll **have** to **probe** the **gar**den,
A **task** that **I** dis**dain**.

But **next** year **if** I'm **War**den,
It's "**Payments in Advance**",
Ab**scond** with **all** the **mon**ey,
To **live** it **up** in **France**!

A Fifteenth Century John Fray, who was Recorder of the city of London (basically a high court judge), was involved in the allocation of five locations within the city where 'foreign' bakers (those who lived outside the city walls), would be permitted to sell their bread.

> "Friday, 26 April, 4 Henry VI [1426] (The date is incorrectly printed in the Letter-book of the City of London), ordinance by John Mitchell, the Mayor, **John Fray**, the Recorder, John Brokkle, William Gregory, William Estfeld, Thomas Chalton, John Welles, John Hatherle, Stephen Broun, John Gedney, Thomas Wandesford, John Pattesle, John Sutton, John Olney, and Robert Large, Aldermen, that **foreign bakers** bringing foreign bread for sale shall stand at the following five places and not elsewhere, viz., **Billingesgate** and **Quenehithe** with neighbouring vacant places, at **Fletebridge** between the gate of the **common laterine** and the **outer gate of the prision of the Flete** with intervening lane, in Chepe between the High Cross and the **Conduit**, and in Cornhylle between the **Conduit** and Ledynhalle, under penalty of forfeiture of the whole of their foreign bread."

They had selected some of the most unsavoury locations within the city; next to the Thames, at a point where offal from the meat and fish markets were thrown into the river; between the common latrine and the prison; and next to the Conduit, which had become an open sewer! I wonder whether they continued to sale their 'foreign' bread!

I could write a book about the 15th century bakers. There were separate guilds for "White Bakers" and "Brown Bakers". Brown bread was considered to be inferior, but the "Guild of White Bakers" persistently tried to take over the "Guild of Brown Bakers". The "Weights and Measures" inspectors frequently checked that their loaves were not under weight. If convicted for selling under-weight loaves they could be punished by being tied to a hurdle and dragged around the cobble streets.

The 15th century brewing of ciders, ales, and beers, is also worthy of a book. Dutch "beer" was introduced during the 15th century, causing some rivalry between that and English ale. Many labourers were entitled to 8 pints of ale per day as part of their remuneration. Although weaker than modern brews, this quantity probably kept them merry and ready to fight. It may also have been healthier than drinking water.

Drinking water had to be collected from three or four stoups and "fountains" in the city. There were more than 2000 members in the Guild of Water-carriers, and they would frequently fight for the commodity.

My father was a Church Warden and we often provided bed and breakfast for visiting vicars and dignitaries. They usually came during the winter months and I observed that, without exception, they liked a glass of sherry and a warm posterior. We would place chairs round the open fire so that we could all keep warm, but the vicars would always stand to face us, with their backs to the fire. They would rock forwards and backwards on their feet while drinking their sherry and pontificating.

There is the story of one vicar who used to preach "Total Abstinence" quite regularly in his sermons. However, all the choir boys knew that he liked his tipple of Cherry Brandy in the evenings. One year they offered to buy him a bottle as a Christmas present, but only on the condition that he personally thanked them in the pulpit before giving the next sermon. He thought for a moment and then agreed to the deal.

The full complement of choristers attended the following service. They watched in anticipation as he slowly stepped into the pulpit and hesitatingly adjusted his 'dog collar'.

He cleared his throat and said, "Before I begin my sermon I would like to thank our excellent choir, not only for their kind gift of cherries, but also for the spirit in which they were given."

The Buzzard

This poem may appeal to Ornitholog**ists**, Natural**ists**, Motor**ists** and Sentimental**ists**. It was conceived after reading a "poem" in the April 2008 edition of a writers' magazine. That "poem" had been submitted for critical analysis, and I was appalled to find that neither it, nor the edited version, were actually poems. Neither showed any concept of metre, and both can best be described as prose containing an irregular staccato introduced by spacing the words of a sentence down a page. My version was hastily drafted to illustrate how it might have been written as a metred composition. If I had been starting from scratch I might have introduced the story by describing the buzzard soaring in the sky. In that case a dactylic foot might have been more appropriate to emphasize verses such as "**Soar**ing and **soar**ing a**round** in the **sky**".

The subject is close to my heart because, through bad driving, I have killed at least two birds. One was an owl that I hit while driving along a Welsh lane late at night. It looked like a sack lying in the road until it took off just before I made contact. The second was when driving by a lake in France. A duck flew into my windscreen while I was trying to read a notice warning about low-flying water-birds. I will never forget the look of inevitable death in their eyes.

The Buzzard

$$|\, u-u\, |\, u-u\, |\, u-u\, |\, u-u\, |$$
$$|\, u-u\, |\, u-u\, |\, u-u\, |\, u-\, |$$
$$|\, u-u\, |\, u-u\, |\, u-u\, |\, u-u\, |$$
$$|\, u-u\, |\, u-u\, |\, u-u\, |\, u-\, |$$

Majestical **feath**ers des**cend**ing from **heav**en
With **tal**ons ex**tend**ed to **live** and let **die**;
Will **life** be main**tained** by a **life** that is **given**,
When **tal**ons ex**ting**uish that **term**inal **cry**?

With **wings** beating **strong**ly the **buzz**ard as**cend**ed.
A **rabb**it hung **limp**ly, but **tight** in its **grasp**.
Our **path**ways con**verged** there, and **that's** how it **end**ed;
Run **down** by cold **met**al, it **breathed** its' last **gasp**.

The **bod**y ex**pir**ing a**mongst** the lane's **litt**er;
Pul**sa**tions that **peaked** like an **org**asm's **end**.
Its' **amber** eyes **star**ing not **tear**ful or **bitt**er;
Its' **soul** like the **lark** would soon **slow**ly as**cend**.

"A *voyeur* of **mur**der", I **pon**dered while **kneel**ing,
And **I** was the **one** who com**mitt**ed the **crime**.
My **car** was a **pawn** in my **hand** without **feel**ing,
But **I** would re**mem**ber '**till the** **end** of my **time**.

I suspect that you will have found this poem to be much more "poetical" than the previous ones. Once again the stressed syllables have been highlighted so that you can note how the stanzas adhere to the somewhat difficult metre. The last verse of the final stanza contains an irregularity that requires "'till the" to be read as a single unstressed syllable. You may also note that the second and fourth verses (lines) of each stanza appear to end with an iambic foot. If you want to be pedantic, and comply with the rest of the stanza, this iambic foot could be described as a catalectic amphibrachic foot.

The Palæolithic or Old Stone Age

I have always been interested in Archaeology, particularly Pre-Historic Archaeology and Palaeolithic art. It ties in well with my other hobbies of Speleology, Geology, History, and Art. I have visited most of the Pre-Historic Caves in France and Spain, but I really got hooked on Palaeolithic Art after reading a book entitled "On the Track of Prehistoric Man" by Herbert Kühn. It contained a picture of deer and fish, reproduced from an engraving.

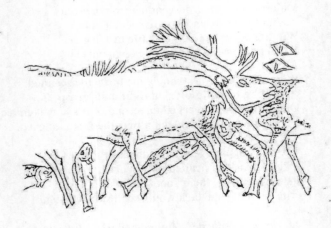

The original sculpture was engraved about 14,000 years ago in-the-round on a piece of bone about 7 inches long. The reproduction was obtained by rolling the bone on a prepared surface. It was merely described as "An Engraving of Deer and Fish", but another book that reproduced the same figure, suggested that the fish were salmon. Neither author could decide whether the diamond-shaped objects were intended to be bubbles or lumps of rock.

I have suggested[*] that the engraving holds more information than is at first apparent. The last deer is looking back and gives the impression of being chased. The middle deer is clearly swimming because the hind legs can not be bearing weight, and traces of the antlers appear to lie along its back, which would be the case if the nostrils are out of the water. The hind legs of the front deer hang limply downwards, which may be intended to indicate that it is dead. I therefore interpret the engraving as portraying a deer hunt in which the deer

---

[*] Hereford Caving Club Newsletter; No 41; December 1987; pp 18-22.

24

are driven into water, such as a lake or river, where they will be slow-moving and can be bombarded with large stones from the cliff-top, instead of wasting carefully worked flint arrow-heads or spear-heads.

I mentioned this to two professors when I attended an International Conference on Palæolithic Art at Oxford University. They were sceptical of the interpretation because it was *in vogue* to believe that ALL art was done for religious reasons by Prehistoric Sharmen, and I was suggesting that it was illustrative of a hunting scene, and might have been a teaching aid.

More recently, a French University student who was my personal guide for a visit to "Grottes de Nieux", got quite excited by my interpretation. I also pointed out to him that the engraver was probably able to swim, or else he would not have been able to picture the leg arrangement of the front two deer. What do you think?

A cave painting that I find particularly appealing also depicts deer swimming in a river. Although not so well executed as some paintings, this artist has shown a great deal of imagination by exploiting a mottled band on the passage wall as the river for the painting. To me this effort seems much more like "Art for Art's Sake" rather than the product of a Shaman in a trance. If you were a Palæolithic hunter on a cold winter day and had caught sufficient food for the tribe, what would you do? I would have gone into a cave to get out of the bad weather; repaired or made new clothing and hunting tools; and amused myself and the older children by painting or teaching them about animals and how to hunt.

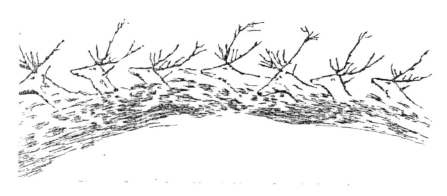

The poem was written after watching "Time Team" on television, but any impression that characters in this poem may have been based upon Mike Aston, Philip Harding, Stewart Ainsworth, John Gater, Victor Ambrus, and Tony Robinson is fairly strongly denied!

25

The Palæolithic or Old Stone Age

As the metre in this poem is fairly strong, it has not been highlighted.

| u - | u - | u - | u - | etc..

When primates clambered down from trees
They found that they could walk with ease
On TWO legs through the forest floor
Instead of using up all four,
And that allowed their other pair
To hold and carry, break or tear.
So using rocks and lumps of wood
They had the strength and tools that could
Compete with claw and Sabre-tooth,
Or dig out traps for horn and hoof.

Primeval men were much alike;
But Wart and Jo and Ding and Ike
Were rather bright and learnt to fuse
Their single syllables, and use,
Instead of "ug" or "dit" and "er"
Or "so" and "all" or "it" and "fur",
Some longer word that seemed to fit
Like "so-dit-all" and "ug-er-it".
But Ding would use vernacular;
Instead of "er" he would say "ar".

The old and greying Ike had thought
That speech, and hunting, should be taught.
So near the middle of our land
He built a hut to house this band.
(It's now a University
And "Stone Age" is an Arts degree.)
The ancient students learned to clonk
A bird or mammal on its conk,
And use new words like "ug-er-all".
(Things haven't really changed at all!)
The Lecturer (Ike's brilliant choice)
Was fleet of foot, with chirpy voice.
They called him "toe knee" "Robin-song"
And he could chirp for three days long.

Now Geo Jo and Tracker Wart
Would tell old Ike just where he ought
To dig a pit to trap the prey.
Old Ike would think, and then relay
This data to young Robin-song,
Who'd turn and tell it to the throng.
Then Victor with his petraglyphs
Recorded it upon the cliffs.
But when it came to dig the thing
They had to call in Master Ding.
He'd dig the hole, and when he'd done
He'd go and dig another one!
Once Master Ding got in his stride
Holes kept appearing far and wide.
And when he wasn't digging those
He'd stop to knap, but not repose .....
He found that knapping stones to bits
Helped him relax from digging pits.
The heavy stones were much reduced
By all the flakes that Ding produced.
Remaining cores were much too light
To give a beast that fatal smite;
And shards that Ding had left around
Made painful walking on the ground.
Apart from making Ike's feet sore
He was rebuked for one thing more.
He seldom stopped to fill pits in,
Which Ike had called "a *mort*-all sin".
So frequently they'd hear Ike say
"Go <u>fill</u>-it Ar Ding, right away.
And killing-stones should all be mint.
They are no use as bits of flint!"
To stop these stones from being cut
Ike hid them all within his hut,
So older students had the gall
To say he lived in "A-Stone" Hall.
They learnt techniques for killing game,
But pale-faced Leonard came to fame
Because his learning skills were poor.
What's more he hated blood and gore.
He wouldn't bonk deer on the head;
But tried to feed them stones instead!

So other students thought him thick
And handed him a lot of stick.
One day, confronted by a bear,
He didn't run or turn a hair,
But ducked beneath its flaying paw
And stuffed Ding's flints into its jaw.

By now I think you ought to see
The reason Stone Age come to be.
It's not through Ar Ding knapping flint,
Nor Ike, ensuring stones were mint ....

| u u - | u u - | u u - | u u - | etc..

I will **have** to change **me**tre to **help** me ex**plain**
How this **Age** of Pre**hist**'ry has **got** its strange **name**.
Though you **prob**-ab-ly **thought** that my **name** for this **age**
Would be **based** on the **gray**ing old **stone**-hording **sage**,
I will **now** let you **know** I've been **tak**ing the **mick**,
It's that **dim**-witted **stu**dent "Pale-**Leo**-the-**Thick**"!

There is some evidence that Palaeolithic man did aim arrows or spears at the mouth of a bear, as indicated in a 17,000 year old wall engraving at *Les Trois Freres*, and it would be natural to aim for the mouth of any animal that was charging towards you.

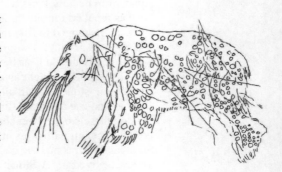

An exception might be a rhinoceros. In that case you would try to get out of its path and aim at its belly. There are same ivory carvings found at Vogelherd in southern Germany that seem to indicate the best places to aim for on different animals. I have suggested that they may have been teaching aids for "Junior"[1].

The carving of a rhinoceros has hatching along the side of its belly, which is about the only region where a flint arrow or spear would have any hope of penetrating.

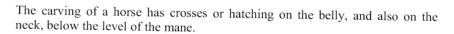

The carving of a horse has crosses or hatching on the belly, and also on the neck, below the level of the mane.

[1]Hereford Caving Club Newsletter No 42; December 1988; pp 9-14.

A mammoth would have presented a major problem. It could not be attacked from the front, and its' belly had long hair that would be difficult to penetrate

with an arrow or spear. I used to be an archer, and during the winter I would shoot indoors over a range of 50 foot, using old canvass hose-pipes as a backcloth. At that range I could shoot an arrow straight through one side of a paint tin, and out the other side, despite the fact that my wooden bow only had a draw weight of about 40lb. However, if an arrow hit the flexible canvass it would just bounce off. Palæolithic man, by experience, would have discovered that it was not a good idea to shoot at the regions where there was long fur.

The carving of a mammoth seems to concur with this. It has crosses scratched down its' back, but above the belly and near the region where there the ribs are smaller. It also has crosses across the shoulder behind the back of the ear, but in front of the rather small scapula.

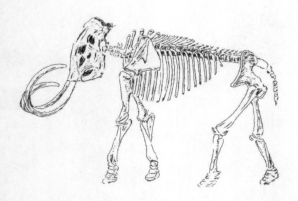

Here's How to Paint the Modern Way

This painting was included to show a 'hake'. In art, a hake is not a fish, but a flat paintbrush of a form similar to that depicted on the right. If you bought the colour version of this book you can note that the painting also illustrates the use of complementary colours (orange-yellow is complementary to purple-blue), and the use of opposite tones (light against dark, and dark against light). The painting was also achieved using a very limited palette of colours.

The other term that you might need to know before reading the poem is "scrumble". You probably won't find it in a dictionary, but it describes a technique used when a water-colour artist changes a colour by rubbing in a new colour on top of the pre-existing colour. Normally the pre-existing colour would be moistened using a fairly stiff brush, so that the reconstituted paint can be lifted off with a dry tissue, but some pigments are staining, and cannot be removed by that technique. 'Scrumbling' quite often leaves the worked area looking very dead and 'muddy'.

Classical painters endeavoured to make a painting look as realistic as possible, but Turner may have been the first British painter to leave more to the imagination. Joseph Mallord William Turner was born on the 23rd April 1775. His father was a barber. That may appear to be a low-income occupation, but in those days a barber often undertook minor surgical operations, and therefore he did have some status in society. He was able to get Joseph into the Royal Academy Schools at the age of 14 years, and at the age of 26 years Joseph became the youngest artist to be elected as a Royal Academician. He seems to have begun his career by concentrating upon composition rather than reality. He was quite prepared to re-arrange or remove objects from a scene in order to improve the composition, but his water-colour paintings developed in a curious way. He would apply a lot of washes that would loosely define a scene, and then sharpen up the detail using a pen dipped in water-colour paint. After a while he ceased to sharpen the scene in this way. Either he, or his customers, seemed to prefer the paintings when more was left to the imagination. Although he was a prolific oil-painter, his water-colour paintings were actually produced on a production line. He would often have four stretched papers set up at once, each with a pencilled outline of his intended work. Then each paper would be soaked and receive numerous layers of colour, using the wet-into-wet technique.

I don't think that Turner would have described his art as "Abstract", but a Turner Prize is presented every year for any novel form of art that stimulates the imagination. I sometimes wonder what Turner might have thought if he had seen some of the prize winning entries!

This painting of mine, and the one at the end of the poem, would certainly not win the Turner Prize, but I thought that you might find them interesting. Both flowers are close-ups in the style of Georgia O'Keefe, except that I have attempted to paint selected regions in the negative. Consequently complementary colours and opposite tones are automatically adjacent, and each positive or negative region becomes a picture in its own right.

Here's How to Paint the Modern Way

©Adrian F. Fray, February 2007

```
| u - | u - | u - | u - |
  | u - | u- | u - |
| u - | u - | u - | u - |
  | u - | u- | u - |
```

"Here's **How** to **Paint** the **Mod**ern **Way**."
A **novel book** on **art**
That **made** it **look** like **child**'s **play**.
I **really had** to **start**.

On **holiday**, quite **near** the **coast**,
The **views** were **really great**.
A **painting here** could **let** me **boast**
A **hanging in** the **Tate**.

I **saw** the **sea** as **Hook**er's **Green**;
The **sky** as **Cobalt Blue**.
The **book implied** that **what** I'd **seen**
Should **be** a **diff'rent hue**.

To **keep** my **paint**ing **loose** is **why**
I **used** my **lar**gest **hake**,
And **when** I **came** to **paint** the **sky**,
I **made** it **Crimson Lake**.

With **Crimson for** the **harb**our **wall**,
The **sea** was **left** to **do**.
I've **tried** to **keep** my **pal**ette **small**,
So **that** was **Crimson too**.

As **yellow boats** looked **out** of **place**
With **sails** of **bril**<u>l</u>iant **white**,
I **crim**soned-**up** the **sail**ing **race**;
Removing **it** from **sight**!

"You **must** stand **back** to **view** your **art**."
Is **what** the **text**book **said**.
But **now** that **textbook's torn** a**part**,
For **all** I **saw** was **red**!

33

I **read**, before I **tore** the **book**,
  A **tip** that's **element**'ry.
"To **give** your **work** a **stun**ning **look**
  Use **col**ours **complement**ary."

So **look**ing **at** my **col**our **guide**,
  I **chose** an **Em**erald **Green**,
And **scrum**bled **it** from **side** to **side**
  Until no **red** was **seen**.

Be**cause** it **looked** like khaki **mud**,
  I **lab**elled **it** "Disguise".
And **sent** it **to** the **Lon**don **Tate** —
  It's **won** "The **Tur**ner **Prize**"!

Coleford Iron Mines

Many of my early caving trips were to the Forest of Dean. In 1961, my first wife, Doreen, found some clay crucibles in a spoil-heap. They were about two inches in diameter and were obviously a crude form of lighting. The remains of wax in the hollow top had been nibbled away by a small rodent whose tooth-marks could still be clearly seen. On the sides were triangular-sectioned holes where pieces of wood had been inserted to support the lamps. I gave these to Peter Standing of the Gloucester Speleological Society, and they are now exhibited in the Clearwell Show Caves/Mines at Coleford. The Clearwell Show Caves were the brain-child of Ray Wright, a founder member of the Royal Forest of Dean Caving Club. During the weeks leading up to Christmas the Caves/Mines are decorated as a Father Christmas Grotto.

Doreen looking down one of the entrances to a Coleford Iron Mine.

Coleford Iron Mines

```
| u u - | u u - |
| u u - | u u - |
 | u u - | u u - | u u - | u ... |
| u u - | u u - |
| u u - | u u - |
 | u u - | u u - | u u - | u ... |
```

'Though the **For**est of **Dean**
May ap**pear** very **green**,
   That is **on**ly when **viewed** from the **sur**face.
If you **dig** a big **hole**
You'll find **och**re and **coal**
   To make **ir**on or **steel** in your **fur**nace.

When the **Brit**ons scraped **scowles**
With their **ant**ler-tip **trowels**,
   They were **hop**ing to **look** quite dram**at**ic.
As the **red** of the **ores**
Would be **rubbed** in their **pores**
   To make **fac**es look **strange**ly hae**mat**ic.

When the **Rom**ans ar**rived**
They were **ver**y sur**prised**
   That the **ir**on was **used** for our **coin**age
Our in**fla**tion in **pay**
As it **rust**ed a**way**
   Was re**duc**ing their **prof**it from **pill**age.

And they **want**ed some **slaves**
When they **mined** Coleford **caves**
   Where the **ore** was an **aqua**-depos**it**.
So we **did**n't re**lent**
When these **for**eigners **went**
   But we **raised** up our **fists** and said "*prosit*".

Making **plough**shares and **swords**
For the **peas**ants and **lords**
   Kept the **ore** econom**ic** for **min**ing;
But hard **times** were a**head**
As they **went** in the **red**
   'though the **lodes** of red **ore** were de**clin**ing.

They were **left** to the **bat**
To the **fox** and the **rat**,
   Until **cav**ers be**gan** to ex**plore** them.
As the **cav**ers had **drinks**
A thought-**bub**ble said "**Thinks!**
   A Mus**eum** would **help** us re**store** them.

So we **won't** mine the **ore**
We'll just **open** the **door**
   When the **vis**itors **queue** to get **in**;
And to **make** it more **fun**
Father **Christ**mas can **come**
   And give **pres**ents to **those** without **sin!**"

So when **Christ**mas is **near**
If your **con**science is **clear**
   And you **come** here to **vis**it his **grot**to,
You should **think** of the **Brits**,
The Free-**min**ers in **pits**,
   And those **cav**ers who **drunk** themselves **blot**to!

This story concerns a deceased friend named Innett Homes. Innett had been an Agricultural Engineer in partnership with someone named Jones, and they traded under the title "Homes and Jones, Agricultural Engineers". Innett specialized in the electrical side of agricultural engineering. In particular he used to repair or install heating for the Herefordshire hop kilns. It is for that reason that he had the nickname "Sparky Homes". His partner used to specialize on the mechanical items and repair tractors and other engines. Consequently local farmers had nicknamed him "Piston Jones". Innett and I were talking about agricultural engineering during one of our caving trips. Suddenly Innett changed the topic.

"Aye, Aye, did you know that Jones had his nickname long before he and I started our partnership?"

"No.", I replied.

"Aye, Aye", he said, "it goes right back to his courting days. He and his lady friend were lying down by the hedge in a field near Ledbury when a car stopped in the road on the other side. A man got out and ran over to the hedge, and that, Adrian, is when he got his nickname! Aye Aye." He turned to me and smiled.

The Iron Age

An Iron Mine that I have visited on a number of occasions is Taff's Well, in South Wales. This photo shows cavers looking into a water-filled shaft in the mine. I was going to use this photo as a basis for a serious poem about archaeology in mines, but I got carried away, and wrote one of my silly "Not Just So" stories. A female character in the poem uses the same "Aye, aye" expression as Innett Homes.

Iron is found in many rocks and minerals, but the ores that are most frequently mined are Hematite and Limonite. Both of these are oxides of iron, but Limonite is a hydrated form. A carbonate of iron called Siderite is also mined, but the concentration of iron in it is low. Iron also forms several different sulphides, such as Pyrrhotite, Marcasite, and Pyrite, but these are primarily mined for their sulphur content.

Hematite can vary from being a hard dark mineral to a soft red powder. Its' name, Hematite, is derived from the Greek word *hema*, meaning blood, but it is frequently called "red-ochre". The hydrated form, Limonite, is an earthy yellow colour, and that is frequently called "yellow-ochre". In the Clearwell Cave/Mine these ores are still mined for artists' pigments.

Cast iron, although hard, is quite brittle. It was not until 1856 that a process for manufacturing steel was initiated by Sir Henry Bessemer.

The Iron Age

| u - | u - | u - | u - |
        etc..

In days of yore, when Britons strode
Attired in furs and daubed with woad,
A wench who lived in Southern Wales
Tried every trick to catch her males.
Her name was Rhonda Mear, and she
Had sister Bess and brother Lee.
Self-centred and with diction poor
Her sentences had "I's" galore,
And "Aye" was used instead of "Yes",
Which did annoy her sister Bess.
She'd look at Rhon and with a sigh
Ask if she meant "Eye", "Aye", or "I"!
Then brother Lee, while being terse,
Nick-named her "Aye" which made it worse.
"Dear sister Aye", he said one day,
"Have many males 'cum bye' your way ?".
(He herded sheep and that is why
He used strange words like 'cum' and 'bye'.)
"Aye, aye", said Rhon, "I've had a batch,
But none thought I was up to scratch.
I've dated every male named Jones
But all of them were just like clones.
They thought that I was much too tall
And couldn't see my face at all.
By dating them it's taken years
And cost a lot in time and tears.
I've started on the men named Smith
And currently I'm passed the fifth,
But Harry, Bruce, and Mike, and Dell
Have all decided that I smell.
Their uncle Jim was very nice,
But thought my fur was full of lice.
So none of them stayed long with me."
"Why don't you have a bath?" said Lee.
"And maybe you should change your fur
To give yourself renewed allure!"

39

"Aye, aye", said Rhon, "I'll change my wear,
Instead of elk I could go 'bear',
Or have two moles upon my chest
And just use hares to hide the rest!"
"That's fine." said Lee, "You could look great,
And ought to catch a worthy mate,
But all the flesh you now expose
Is blue with wode from head to toes."
"Aye, aye, I don't like blue." she said.
I think I'll try some ochre red,
And rub it over ALL of me."
"Without the use of skins?" asked Lee.
"I think that skins collect the lice,
And when they're old they don't smell nice."

So bared of all but natural skin,
With just the ochre red rubbed in,
She walked around in that attire
Which set the hom'id world afire.
For all the males flocked round to say
"We like the skin you wear today."
And thus she met a Smith named Blake,
Who baked the bread, hence "Smith-the-Bake".
This Smith was from the Upper Crust
So catching him would be a MUST.
She realized that she HAD allure
When she found he kneaded her.
He thought the colour of her red
Reminded him of crusty bread.
So naturally they joined as one
And she began to bake his bun.

Meanwhile the winter nights drew in,
And Rhonda craved a warmer skin,
But Blake still liked her bare attire
So baked her ochre in his fire.
"Your ochre melts!" he said to Rhon.
"Aye, aye," she said, "my ochre's gone!"

This ochre-bake was named by Lee.
He called the metal "Aye-Rhon", see!
So that is how it all began.
Rhon's husband was the "Blake-Smith" man;

40

Improvements later would appear
And those were done by "Bessy-Mear".
So, did the Iron Age begin
When Rhon rubbed ochre on her skin?

Pre-historic men probably painted their bodies with red-ochre and yellow-ochre, but you may also be interested to know that red-ochre, oak bark, animal brains, and urine were used to preserve skins after fat had been scraped off the inside. Any residual fat could turn rancid, thereby producing the obnoxious smell that might have persuaded Rhon to rub ochre over herself, instead of wearing animal skins!

In 1856 Sir Henry Bessemer described and patented a cheap process for removing or reducing many of the impurities in 'pig' iron, such as carbon, silicon, manganese, sulphur, and phosphorous. Pure iron would be relatively brittle, but the retention of very small quantities of certain of these impurities is used to produce various grades of steel.

Forging steel at Morgan's Blacksmith workshop, Malvern.

Jack and the Beanstalk

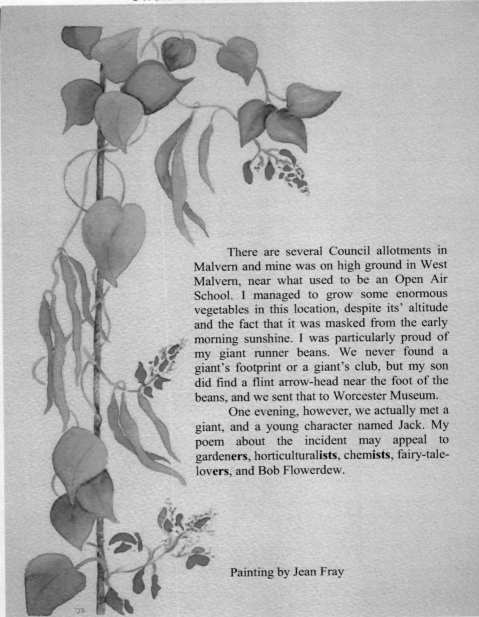

There are several Council allotments in Malvern and mine was on high ground in West Malvern, near what used to be an Open Air School. I managed to grow some enormous vegetables in this location, despite its' altitude and the fact that it was masked from the early morning sunshine. I was particularly proud of my giant runner beans. We never found a giant's footprint or a giant's club, but my son did find a flint arrow-head near the foot of the beans, and we sent that to Worcester Museum.

One evening, however, we actually met a giant, and a young character named Jack. My poem about the incident may appeal to gardeners, horticulturalists, chemists, fairy-tale-lovers, and Bob Flowerdew.

Painting by Jean Fray

Jack and the Beanstalk

u -	u -	u -	u -
u -	u -	u -
u -	u -	u -	u -
u -	u -	u -

West Malvern, where the Council let
  Allotments to the keen
Or wife-avoiding gardening set,
  Is where I grew the bean.

And that is where I met with Jack,
  And with a giant too,
Who stood beside my giant bean
  That grew and grew and grew.

The bean was by the central path,
  The last one in the row.
The giant clasped a giant staff,
  And Jack was held in tow.

The giant looked me in the eye,
  "I like your giant bean.
It must be twice as tall as I,
  The biggest I have seen.

This footpath's on my homeward way,
  So when I'm striding through
I stop to see it every day,
  And hoped to talk to you."

He asked me why it grew so well,
  And said he'd like to know
If I had used a magic spell
  To make it grow and grow.

"Someone here keeps wat'ring it,
  Often with a spray,
And that is what has altered it.
  It happens every day.

This person who has not been seen.
   Perhaps has used a hose,
And let it drain against the bean.
   There's no one here that knows."

"And did he also use manure
   To make it grow so green?",
The giant said, and pulled Jack's fur,
   "Don't touch the gard'ner's bean."

But Jack the Russell sniffed at it,
   And we began to see
That what we'd thought was H_2O,
   Was really K_9P.

The moral of this story is,
   The reason why it grew
Was Jack had watered it with piss.
   Like Robert Flowerdew!

Before I acquired the allotment it had been used by someone who reared pigs.
No doubt that was the reason for my giant beans!

Felicide

This poem is based upon Blake's poem entitled "The Tiger". William Blake was born in London on the 28th November 1757. His father was a Hosier, and it was William's eldest brother, James Blake, who succeeded their father in the family business. William had shown some artistic ability so he was sent to an "Art" school, and then apprenticed to an engraver. After completing his apprenticeship he initially made a living as an engraver, but subsequently became a prolific artist and poet, thanks to some useful contacts and an artistic wife. Many of his paintings, engravings and poems are of a religious or mystic nature, and this has led some people to suppose that he had a mental problem, perhaps induced by lead and various toxic chemicals he encountered when engraving and painting.

His most famous poem comes from his Preface to "Milton". It became the hymn whose first stanza begins "And did those feet in ancient times". Probably "The Tiger", from "Songs of Experience", is a close second. It is only when writing my parody of "The Tiger" that I noticed the metre of the last verse in each stanza is not consistent from stanza to stanza. Analyze his verses and you'll see what I mean:-

"Could **frame** thy **fearful symmetry**?"

"**What** the **hand** dare **cease** the **fire**?"

"**What** dread **hand** and **what** dread **feet**?"

"**Dare** in **deadly ter**rors **clasp**?"

"Did **he** who **made** the **Lamb** make **thee**?"

"Dare **frame** thy **fearful symmetry**?"

I have been careful to maintain an identical metre in each stanzas based upon the metre of his first stanza.

Felicide

```
| - u | - u | - u | -      a
| - u | - u | - u | -      a
| - u | - u | - u | - |    b
  | u - | u - | u - | u - |    b
```

Tiger, tiger burning bright,
Now I've got you in my sight
I will fire by three-o-three,
   And blast you to eternity.

Every day I use my gun.
Finding it enormous fun
Killing all your kith and kin
   To fill my fifty rooms with skin.

None of you is left to waste.
Every bone is ground to paste.
Eastern countries pay me well,
   To use this potion as a spell.

Ladies like to strut and gloat,
Showing off your golden coat.
Gentlemen's baronial halls
   Display your head upon their walls.

As your tiger numbers dropped,
Scarcity when ladies shopped
Made your skin cost even more,
   Which made me richer than before.

Now I think a year has past
Since I shot and skinned the last.
Recounting this I'll be succinct,
   Tiger, tiger, you're extinct.

Forests where you used to roam,
Ceased to function as your home.
Natives found that they can earn
    A living, if they slash and burn.

Tiger, tiger, snuffed out right
Like your forests of the night.
What a stupid prat was I
    To frame your fearful symmetry.

Bengal Tigers normally have a bright tawny-yellow fur with dark stripes, but some carry a regressive gene that is capable of producing offspring with white fur, as shown in this photo. In the event of an Ice Age, this could become a dominant gene.

LASER

The name LASER is an acronym for **L**ight **A**mplification by the **S**timulated **E**mission of **R**adiation. The original acronym was for **M**icrowave **A**mplification by the **S**timulated **E**mission of **R**adiation (MASER). The latter genuinely is an amplifier, but the former, although using the same basic principles, is used as a source (i.e. a radiator). Although it uses the term "Light", there are LASERS that emit infra-red and ultra-violet radiation. These radiators can be made from certain types, or mixtures of gases; certain types of semi-conductor configurations; and certain crystalline materials containing specific impurities. None of this will have made you any wiser unless you understand what is meant by "Stimulated Emission", and I will endeavour to explain this in terms of a crystalline LASER.

Most of you will be aware of the concept of negatively charged electrons orbiting around a positively charged nucleus, rather like planets orbiting a sun. That is merely a simplistic way to appreciate what happens. Electrons have another attribute we term "spin", and the rotating charge makes them behave like magnetic dipoles. These will interact with one another, particularly when two or more elements combine to form a compound. Under those conditions the concept of an orbit becomes meaningless, and it is mathematically easier to describe electrons as occupying "energy levels". Electrons will populate the lowest energy levels first, and there will be fewer in the higher levels (The population decreases exponentially). The frequency of electromagnetic radiation is proportional to its energy. If a frequency corresponding to the energy difference ($e_2 - e_1$) is incident upon this crystal, it will be absorbed as it raises electrons from e_1 to e_2 (or be amplified if they drop from e_2 to e_1).

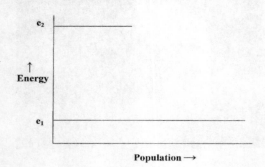

Eventually the two levels will become equal, and surplus energy will pass through as though the crystal was transparent. The secret of a LASER is to devise a way by which e_2 is greater than e_1. Under those conditions the incident beam will be amplified as it stimulates electrons to equate between the two levels. If the crystal is situated between two mirrors there will be "positive feedback", and that will convert the amplifier into an oscillator (or source). In order to allow it to radiate, one of the mirrors is manufactured to be slightly less than 100% reflecting. Light bouncing between the two mirrors stimulates the electrons to drop down "in phase" with one another, and that means the radiation will be "coherent". As the radiation is at a single frequency (i.e. monochromatic), and it is also coherent, it will produce a powerful beam with very little divergence.

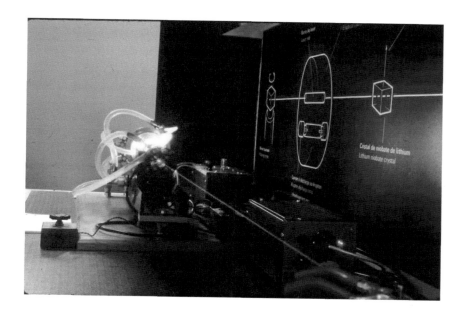

The LASER crystal in the photograph actually produces infra-red radiation, but I placed a special "non-linear" crystal in the cavity with it. That crystal is able to double the frequency and that is why you can see a green beam. Not so complicated is it?

Compare the slightly different metre between "Laser" and the previous poem.

LASER

```
| u - | u - | u - | u - |      a
| u - | u - | u - | u - |      a
| u - | u - | u - | u - |      b
| u - | u - | u - | u - |      b
```

Oh Laser, Laser, burning bright,
You're Infra Red so out of sight,
And yet your thermal ray is felt
By distant targets, as they melt.

Coherently, your narrow beam
Does not diverge, so it would seem
Your energy will concentrate,
So you can cut through metal plate.

More reasons for extolling you,
Are you can cut ceramics too,
And if you cut through cloth or plaid
You fuse the edge, unlike a blade.

Oh Laser, Laser, burning bright,
I wonder if your I.R. light
Could turn into an optics tool
If I could make you visible.

A crystal in your cavity,
If lacking linearity,
Would double up I.R. to green,
And make a light that can be seen.

It worked and gave a brilliant beam,
But that is all, for it would seem
An Optics Tool was just a dream,
So Government dispersed the team.

This green LASER was demonstrated on a British Stand at the Paris Air Show in 1967, but the research was disbanded for economic reasons after we returned to England. Consequently the experimental results were never published!

Pant Mawr Pot

Pant Mawr Pot was an exhausting challenge in the days when one could only enter it by carrying a heavy ladder and belay line across the moor, and I wondered whether I would ever go down it another time.

Laddering the pot on a cold winter morning.

Some of the party in the main chamber.

I have written this poem without rhyme, using the same metre as *Hiawatha*. It was surprisingly difficult to maintain stress on the first syllable and no stress on the last syllable of each verse (line).

Some of the excellent straw formations.

The Cascade.   The entrance ladder pitch.

Pant Mawr Pot

| - u | - u | - u | - u |

Snow was lying on the heather,
Thinly on the moorland heather,
Thinly, crisply on the heather.
Ice encrusted pathway puddles
Cracked beneath our heavy footsteps.
Cavers acting just like children
Throwing stones at greenhouse windows,
Shattered puddles into pieces.
And the noise of stone-cracked puddles
Broke the silence of our voices.

All awhile the day was breaking.
Watery sunlight dawned upon us
As we reached the gaping chasm.
Awe inspiring was the chasm,
Dropping from the chilly moorland
To the hidden cave beneath us.
Some just sat in contemplation,
Others got equipment ready;
Ready for the great adventure.
Ladder-lengths were joined together.
Joined and tested three-times over.
Then unrolled into the darkness,
Hanging from a prayed-for skewer.
Well-belayed I gripped the ladder,
Trusting that my friends above me
Wished to have me back among them.
Back to write more lewd poems.
Poems that might well offend them!

Down Pant Mawr the rest descended,
Climbing down a clinking ladder,
Clinking with a sweet reminder,
"I'm of metal and will hold you.
I'll be here to help you exit."
Then we gathered in main chamber;
Where we stood and gazed in wonder.
Fascinated by its grandeur.

Stalactites were in profusion,
Clinging to the night-sky ceiling.
Stalactites whose whiteness glistened;
Wetted by their tear-drops dripping,
Raising from the rocks beneath them
Stalagmites who strove to meet them.
Infant straws were there in clusters.
Helictites with indecision
Tried to grow in all directions.
Whilst the roar of water falling
Echoed round the black stone-walling.

Then we looked down every passage.
Looked in every nook and cranny;
Clambered over every boulder;
Sought to pass the sump that stopped us.
Sought to find a virgin chamber
Where "Man Friday's" rubber wellies
Hadn't left their moulded footprint.
But alas there was no opening.
Nowhere here was worthwhile digging.
So we moved back to the entrance.
Looked up to the fresh-air entrance;
Saw the re-assuring ladder
Life-lined to the dappled moonlight.
Tired legs were glad to reach it.
Climbing ladders is exhausting.

Walking back with heart fast beating,
Throbbing with the thrill of "doing",
And my mind switch on to dreaming;
Thinking of Pant Mawr beneath me.
Thinking that there were so many
Other places well worth seeing;
Here at home or foreign countries.
Other things I could be doing,
Learning, making, writing, painting.
Going down Pant Mawr was thrilling,
But, with other things to tempt me,
Would this be my only visit?
I must cherish and remember
Pant Mawr Pot, this cold December!

Vallum

In this poem I wanted to use the Latin words *sinister dexter* (left, right), but *sinister* has a stressed and two unstressed syllables and there is no way in which one can force this emphasis to be changed. Consequently it is impossible to include this word in a poem that uses the iambic foot. I could have used the dactylic foot, the amphibrach foot or a combination of dactylic and trochaic feet. The latter would have given a good impression of marching soldiers, "*sinister dexter*, *sinister dexter*, *sinister dexter*, *sinister dexter*", but would not have been appropriate for the rest of the poem, so I settled on the anapaestic foot. This is a difficult metre to maintain, because the first two syllables of a verse (line) have to be unstressed. You need to be aware of the intended metre, and may have to read the poem two or three times before it begins to flow.

Hadrian's Wall

The Amphitheatre in Rome.

The surface in the amphitheatre upon which events took place is represented by the white area in the lower photo. Beneath this arena can be seen a series of passageways, rooms, and even lifts. The Romans had the ability to astonish spectators, and combatants by having animals as large as elephants pop up into the arena! What is more, the arena was sufficiently watertight for the surface to be flooded so that mock sea battles could be enacted.

Vallum

```
| u u - | u u - | u u - | u u - |  a
| u u - | u u - | u u - | u u - |  a
| u u - | u u - | u u - | u u - |  b
| u u - | u u - | u u - | u u - |  b
```

When the **Em**peror **Had**rian **land**ed in **Kent**
He re**vea**led a grand **scheme** upon **which** he was **bent**.
"It's a **hun**dred whole **years**, or per**haps** a bit **more**,
Since we **Ro**mans in **le**gions in**va**ded this **shore**.

This mo**ment**ous **e**vent we can **all** cele**brate**,
And we'll **build** a grand **struc**ture to **show** we are **great**.
We will **build** a long **wall** from the **east** to the **west**,
And we'll **build** it up **north** where the **dist**ance is **less**."

When his **gen**'rals heard **this** they all **gasped** with sur**prise**,
And they **asked** their dear <u>**Hadr'an**</u> if he **thought** that was **wise**.
They said "**Is** there a **rea**son for **choo**sing a **wall**?
For we **real**ly can't **see** any **us**es at **all**!

Don't you **think** it more **pru**dent to **build** a big **dome**,
And to **make** it out-**stage** Amphi**thea**tres in **Rome**?
It could **shel**ter our **le**gions, when **want**ing to **train**,
During **cold** British **sum**mers with in**ces**sant **rain**."

"It's the **Wall**.", said their **Em**peror, "**Let** us set **forth**,
And re**gen**erate **roads** while we're **mar**ching up **north**."
They sang "*sinister dexter*" in **time** with their **tread**
Thinking "*stolidus vallum*", more **like**ly, in**stead**!

They com**plet**ed the **wall** and they **built** the **A1**,
But in **two** thousand **years** a full **cir**cle has **come**.
For we **now** have a **dome** with no **us**es at **all**
And should **real**ly have **built** a pro**tec**tive sea **wall**!

57

The Bronze Age

Bronze is an alloy of copper and tin. It should not be confused with Brass, which is an alloy of copper and zinc. Bronze is a rather dull grey/green yellow when it is untarnished, whereas brass is a brighter yellow. Pure copper is a malleable metal, unsuitable for most tools or weapons, but the two alloys are much harder and bronze, in particular, can be used for knives and swords.

Current research indicates that Bronze was initially produced in the Middle-East about 6,000 years ago, but as far as the United Kingdom is concerned, the Bronze Age dates from about 2,300 years BC, and ends with the beginning of the Iron Age in about 700 BC. Cooking during the Bronze Age was usually done in ceramic (clay) pots, and not copper pots as stated in the poem. Large bronze cauldrons would have been quite difficult to manufacture. Some of the largest Bronze Ages pots were made in China. There is also the Jinju Pot, found in Korea, and other reasonably large vessels in Eastern Europe and India. There is a smaller ornate bronze pot in the British Museum.

Supposing that Bronze Age people had been able to manufacture a very large copper cauldron, they would still have needed to fit a bronze handle because a copper one would have bent under the weight of its contents.

The development of farming and the building of wooden or stone Henges did occur during the Bronze Age, so, in that respect my "Just So" poem does have a ring of truth!

I hope that it may appeal to Archaeologists, Farmers, the W. I., and Old Age Pensioners.

The Bronze Age

| u - | u - | u - | u - |
etc..

When hunting game with blades of flint
Was commonplace, without a hint
Of growing crops or herding beasts,
Then ALL the meals were meaty feasts.
For what was green, men wouldn't eat;
Nor roots like carrots, turnips, beet.
When gathering these there was no fun;
They couldn't fight or turn and run,
And most of them were tough as skin
Without the taste of meat within.

So Alwyn Lloyd would hunt for game,
His brother George would do the same.
Their mother Bronwyn cooked the meat
That all their tribe would have to eat.
And, 'though her cooking skills were poor,
She'd con her tribe to ask for more
By choosing words that could excite
A Neolithic appetite.
When pork was over-cooked at lunch
She'd say "I've cooked a Crackling Crunch".
If held too high above the flame
"It's Smokey Bacon", she'd exclaim.
And when it didn't fully cook
The Auroch had a "Rare Beef" look.
The time the joint got caked in clay
She did "An Oven Bake" that day.
And when it dropped onto the ash
She didn't swear or look abash,
But thought the mishap really brill',
And called this dish a "Charcoal Grill".
Her husband didn't hunt or cook,
But ate the food and had the look
Of one who kept his belly full.
He was in charge and liked to rule,
And all his tribe on Wiltshire's plains
Accepted Norman as "The Brains".

They were content and quite well fed
Until their George was due to wed.
Nigella Smith, whom he had met,
Had brought her tribe from Somerset,
And now they found it was no myth
That there were lots of folk named Smith!
The tribe called Lloyd could not acquire
Sufficient meat for Bronwyn's fire.
So Bronwyn made synthetic meat
From Onions, Sage, and Emma Wheat.
Bron' stuffed it well inside each beast
And both the tribes enjoyed the feast.
So that is how it came to pass
They ate some roots, some greens, some grass,
And found the taste of these when cooked
Was so much better than they looked.
So Stone Age man began to eat
All sorts of veggies stuffed in meat.
There wasn't really room enough
To fill a beast with so much stuff,
Yet eating meat with mint or sage
And three cooked veg' was all the rage.

Now Norman Lloyd was quick to learn
That veg'tables could help him earn
A Neolithic buck or two,
If Bron could cook them in a stew
Where veg'tables would far exceed
The little bit of meat they need.
But this required a great big pot
Because she'd need to boil a lot.
And that is why their Alwyn beat
A metal pot from copper sheet.
Meanwhile their married son named George
Had joined the Smiths near Cheddar Gorge.
Beside a mere the peat was great
To grow the veg'tables they ate.

At last our Norman built a stall
Where Bron could cook and sell it all,
And yet the name put on display
Was "NORMAN's Gourmet Take-away"!

60

The structure was a wooden ring.
(With Bron as cook, a fatal thing!)
It wasn't long before he found
That she had burnt it to the ground.
So, having said "You silly Crone!",
He built another one of stone,
And Bronwyn found that she was stuck
With helping Norman make a buck.

So he became a wealthy git,
But that is not the end of it,
As from his wealth, you see, there springs
A chain of **N**orman's **G**ourmet rings.
These rings required lots and lots
Of Allwyn's metal cooking pots.
But Allwyn Lloyd was short of ore
When Norman asked him for some more.
So Allwyn made his pots from tin
With quite a lot of copper in,
And Norman's customers were told
The food they ate was cooked in gold!

His women had to cook the meals,
And welcome in, and man the tills.
He dressed them all in see-through skins
And they were named "The **W**elcome **I**ns".
So **N**orman's **G**ourmet Take-Away
Was full of hunters every day!
Because they ate the food George grew,
With sage and onions in their stew,
George found more land, (for crops to boil),
Beyond the mere in drier soil.

To eat the stew and drink the beer.
What Norman charged was just two deer.
But Norman made a solemn pledge
A plated meal with three cooked veg'
Would feature every seventh day
For those old folk who couldn't pay,
And these poor folk of aging years
He called "The Old Sage Pensioners".

By now it should be no surprise

The "Welcome-Ins" were "<u>W I</u>'s".
The cauldron that could hold a lot
The Hunters called an "<u>Al' Lloyd</u>" pot.
And <u>alloyed</u> pots were used to brew
The very tasty "<u>Bron's Sage</u>" stew.
So "<u>Bron's Sage</u>" gourmets learnt to gorge
The vegetables from "<u>Far Mere George</u>".
And these were sold at "<u>Stone N G's</u>",
Where Norman Lloyd collected fees.

So <u>THAT</u> is how Bron's Sage began.
It's just "miss"-spelt by modern man.

Not Stonehenge, but the very impressive Ring of Brodgar Stone Circle and
Henge (embankment with ditch) in Orkney.

Herring Gulls

During the summer of 1955, when I was about 17 years old and just learning to drive, my parents and I drove round Scotland on a camping holiday. I used to take colour slides using an Ilford Advocat camera which was usually loaded with Ilford film. We stopped at a little fishing village called Gourdon so that I could take some photos of the harbour and fishing boats. The poem is based upon the events of that day.

Herring Gulls

```
| u - | u - | u - | u - | u - | u - | u - |
| u - | u - | u - | u - | u - | u - | u - |
| u - | u - | u - | u - | u - | u - | u - |
| u - | u - | u - | u - | u - | u - | u - |
```

The **her**ring **boats**, with **screech**ing **gulls** that **cir**cled **over head**,
Were **chug**ging **in**to **har**bour **where** the **her**ring **gulls** are **fed**.
Each **boat** in **turn** was **moored against** the **weath**ered **gran**ite **quay**.
Erstwhile the **swoop**ing **scav**engers still **squawked** im**pat**iently.

The **lazy ones** began to **perch** up**on** the **har**bour **wall**,
But **non**-the-**less** they **still** re**leased** their **sharp** de**man**ding **call**.
They **watched** the **glist**'ning **silver box**es **pulleyed through** the **hatch**.
They **watched** the **box**es **placed** on **scales** to **weigh** the **scaly catch**.

They **watched** each **box** as **it** ar**rived** be**side** the **gut**ting **slab**,
And **whilst** they **perched** they **thought about** a **has**ty **snatch** and **grab**.
They **watched** two **her**ring **girls** ar**rive**, to**geth**er **with** a **lad**,
With **gut**ting **knives** and **rub**ber **gloves** and **rub**ber **a**prons **clad**.

They **split** the **silver her**rings **read**y **for** the **smo**king **shed**,
And **then** with **off**al **bits** the **her**ring **gulls** were **fed**,
But **still** these **hun**gry **her**ring **gulls** were **seek**ing **more** to **nip**
So **flew away** for **their** de**sert** up**on** the **Coun**cil **tip**.

So **when** you **see** an **oak**-smoked **kip**per **ly**ing **on** your **dish**,
Per**haps** you'll **start** to **won**der **wheth**er **gulls** will **cease** to **fish**.
With **her**rings **dis**ap**pear**ing **this** could **be** the **fi**nal **straw**
That **makes** a **webbed**-foot **fish**ing **bird** e**volve** a **scroun**gers **claw**.

Will's Hole Unvisited

The Hereford Caving Club Coach trips usually started from the Hereford Town Hall. For this trip to Will's Hole the Secretary was generous. In order to save cavers like me having to cycle from Malvern to Hereford; go caving and then cycle back up to Malvern; possibly via the British Camp in rain and with a head-wind; he arranged for the coach to start in Malvern. Unfortunately, it was arranged with the Midland Red Bus Company, and they decided to use a normal bus instead of a coach. Also, for some reason they included a conductress.

It had been snowing before we left Malvern, and the roads were quite slushy. We reached Hereford to pick up the rest of the members and they had great difficulty persuading the driver to continue on his way.

By the time we reached Black Rock it was obvious that we would be unable to complete our journey, but the snowplough had only cleared one lane and there was nowhere for the bus to turn round so it was committed to driving up to Brynmawr.

Most of us, including the dog "Scamp", got out and started walking up the hill, playing silly games on the way.

The snowplough had still not cleared any turning space in Brynmawr. The driver tried backing into the snow but he got stuck and the wheel began to spin. Ian Kelly therefore suggested that the driver could try a handbrake turn in the road in the hope that the back wheels would swing round to the cleared section of road where there was traction. It worked. We were able to drive back down the hill and get home. I was reminded of "The Noble Duke of York" and I wondered whether he had to march his soldiers back down the hill because their route was blocked by snow!

I also began to wonder precisely who the noble or grand old duke of York was intended to be. Some believe that the nursery-rhyme poem was intended to mock Frederick, the second son of George III, who was created duke of York and Albany in 1784. This duke was given command of the British contingent of Colberg's army in Flanders during 1793. Upon his return he was promoted to field-marshal and then commander-in-chief of the British army. Then he was sent to invade Holland, together with a Russian corps. The whole episode was a complete disaster and he had to withdraw. It was evident that he was not a good commander, although he subsequently showed some ability as an organiser. If he was intended to be the butt of a lampoon, then the hill in Holland that his army is supposed to have marched up is probably intended to be part of the pun.

Other people believe that this duke is intended to be Richard III, or his father, Richard of York, but neither of these dukes was old or particularly noble.

The nursery-rhyme poem seems to have initially appeared during 1913 in "Mother Goose". I have not been able to ascertain whether or not it was based upon an older rhyme.

Our day out warranted a poem, but the metre I used to represent the bumpy "bus" ride made the poem rather difficult to complete.

Will's Hole Unvisited

```
| u − u | u − u |
| u − u | u − u |
    | u u - | u u - | u u - |
| u − u | u − u |
| u − u | u − u |
    | u u - | u u - | u u - |
```

The trip in December
Was one I'll remember —
    We intended to visit Wills Hole!
Though not getting to it
The drive put us through it
    Before finishing right up the Pole.

As daylight was breaking
I found myself shaking
    In a cumbersome Midland Red bus.
We had for a driver
A regular skiver
    And he certainly made enough fuss.

" 'sa long way to Brecon",
He said, "An' I reckon
    That the road past Brynmawr will be froze'.
To put it quite plainly",
He said, very sanely,
    "It's a B----- of a day that you've chose'."

At Blackrock we halted,
And as the bus jolted
    To a typical Midland Red stop,
Outside we went sprawling,
So it could start crawling
    Up the slippery road to the top.

Our driver was yearning
The space for a turning,
   Which he thought that Brynmawr would provide.
Whilst we had a calling
For fun with snowballing,
   So decided to walk and not ride.

In kangaroo fashion
Young Scamp showed a passion
   For the snow in the deepest of drifts,
And 'though it was blowing
And faces were glowing
   We thought snow was the best of God's gifts.

Brynmawr, where we faltered,
The road was unaltered,
   And the snow was exceedingly deep.
There wasn't a clearing
So the driver despairing
   Called us back to the bus with a beep.

"I'm worried concerning
The problem of turning
   As the snowplough has just cleared one track.
There isn't the width here
To drive in reverse gear.
   I'll get stuck if I try going back'."

"You could try hand-braking",
Said Ian, "when making
   A quick turn of the wheel when at pace."
So he revved up his engine
And stopped being hemmed in
   As the bus slithered arse about face.

One never stops learning!
For, in about-turning
   I had found what I wanted to know—
Old York wasn't barmy
When reversing his army
   If his hill-top was covered with snow!

All That Jazz

I was born just before the 2nd World War, and brought up on Classical music. Friends and family would gather in our large lounge/dinning-room and play music until late in the evening, about once a month. I was placed in my cot, with a blanket draped around it so that I would not be distracted by what was going on. My eldest brother usually played the piano; other brothers would play their violins, and my father would play the cello or double-bass. During his youth he could play the piano and violin, but he cut his hand badly when he was a trainee butcher, so he taught himself to play these other instruments.

After the War I had piano lessons from an aunt who was a professional pianoforte teacher, having graduated from the London School of Music. I think that I scraped through Grade 1, but was much more interested in "inventing" music rather than practicing set pieces. When I was 11 years' old I went to Grammar school and started to learn the violin. This appealed to me much more than the piano. I also joined all the College societies, including the choir, and took leading (female) roles in the College operas. If I had been able to sing in tune while still at Junior School the headmaster, who was an organist with connections to Winchester College, said that he would have been able to get me a place there. Although I learnt to sing in tune, my sense of rhythm was hopeless .... I could never learn to dance! I continued to play the violin after starting work, until I moved into "digs" where there was an Old English sheepdog. Whenever I took the violin out of its' case, the dog would howl, and hide under the stairs. I have hardly ever played the violin since.

One evening I went to the local theatre and listened to Stéphane Grapelli. He was inspirational! For the first time I could really detect the beat, and realized that Jazz was musical, entertaining, and fun. I also discovered that Jazz musicians drink gallons of beer!

There seem to be several different styles of jazz, but I have never found a satisfactory definition for any of them, although the essential constituent seems to be a strong beat. I have a preference for Traditional Jazz (Trad. Jazz), but that seems to be a misnomer. If jazz is a break-away from traditional music, how can one call it "Traditional Jazz"?

My next poem describes how I believe jazz may have been "invented". I have tried using the same metre as *Vallum*.

69

All That Jazz

```
|u u -|u u -|u u -|u u - |
|u u -|u u -|u u -|u u - |
|u u -|u u -|u u -|u u - |
|u u -|u u -|u u -|u u - |
```

Although **Mur**phy had **tak**en his **ton**ic so **far**
With the **Ir**ish still **stand**ing at **Alistair's Bar**,
He de**cid**ed one **Fri**day to **take** it at **ease**,
So he **sat** at the **up**right, <u>with it</u> **there** on the **keys**.

The **Mu**si**cians** had **gone** for their **cus**tom'ry **break**,
With their **in**struments **left** for drunk **Mur**phy to **take**.
When he **tried** playing **Ver**di he **found** he was **green**,
And the **Fire**works by **Han**del were **not** to be **seen**.

He said "**Mos**hart and **Brug**ner are **not** on my **Lishzt**,
And I **can** not play **Cho**ping when **feel**ing half **pisshed**."
These com**pos**ers must **of**ten have **used** a wrong **note**
As he **sel**dom ad**hered** to the **ones** that they **wrote**.

When the **notes** were com**bined** to con**struct** a long **chord**
He found **sort**ing so **man**y was **mak**ing him **bored**,
But a **sax**ophone **on**ly has **fing**'ring for **one**,
So he **picked** up the **sax**, thinking **that** would be **fun**.

Having **played** for ten **min**utes and **gasp**ing for **air**,
He de**cid**ed the **fid**dle <u>should be</u> **giv**en some **wear**,
But I **think** that its' **strings** were the **guts** of a **cat**
As the **noise** that they **made** seemed to **in**dicate **that**!

He was **used** to a **bar**, so his **rhy**thm was **neat**,
'though he **length**ened some **notes** he main**tained** a strong **beat**.
He would **in**troduce **trills** that were **not** in the **bar**,
And would **some**times re**mem**ber his **ton**ic sol **fa**.

The **Mu**si**cians** re**turned** and they **thought** he was **great**.
They a**greed** that his **rhy**thm was **one** to in**state**.
So you **should**n't be**lieve** that all **drunk**ards are **crass**,
As a **drunk**ard named **Mur**phy in**vent**ed Trad. **Jazz**!

And whenever you **see** Jazz Mu**si**cians at **play**,
You will **note** they bless **Mur**phy <u>in the</u> **time**-honoured **way**.
Their de**vo**tion to **Murphy** <u>is so</u> **firm** and sin**cere**
They con**tinu**'lly **toast** him with **Guin**ness and **beer**!

"Tosh", my landlady's dog that hid under the stairs when I played the violin.

Max – the Any-House Cat

Our neighbours had a black cat that seldom came into our garden when we were around. If it came in not knowing we were there, it would disappear in a flash once it had seen us. It was called Maxwell, after the label on a coffee jar, and its' name was shortened to Max.

One Christmas a boisterous Alsatian puppy was added to the family and Max had nowhere to sleep after a night on the tiles. From that time on, it began to get friendlier and would visit us nearly every day. If we were in the garden and heard the click of the cat-flap, we knew it was on its' way. Incidentally, it was an "it" and not a "him"! It discovered that by wrapping its tail round our legs and trying to trip us up, caused us to issue it with a dish of milk. Sometimes it would even say "Meealk" if we were slow on the uptake. It also discovered that our conservatory was warm and quiet.

About midday it would stretch its legs and ask to leave the conservatory by saying "Meeout", and go into the garden. It wasn't always for the call of nature, so we wondered whether the hard un-cushioned seat in the conservatory was uncomfortable, or whether it was less warm because the sun ceased to shine in soon after midday. Then we spoke to our other neighbours and found that a black cat was also visiting them! They were even more benevolent than us, and started buying tins of cat food for it. After a while it would only stop with us long enough to have a drink, unless those neighbours were away. It had discovered that their conservatory had a cushioned chair and retained the sun until late in the afternoon!

In the twilight of an evening we would see it walk across our front garden on the way home. This was long after it had left this neighbour's house, so where had it been? The answer was that it had been visiting another neighbour further along the road!

Most of the following poem was written during an extended bath! I decided to use a semi-repetitive line (verse) stressing its place of visitation, such as "Our-", "Their-", and "Any-house". Also, almost inadvertently, I found myself using six matching rhymes in each stanza (verse). My poetry master had said that four match rhymes, as in the Lady of Shallot, should not be exceeded because it would be impossible to write several stanzas if using more than four. I have proved him wrong! I wish he was still alive to read it.

Max – the Any-House Cat

©Adrian F. Fray, February 1998

You live next door and use your flap
To come and go to take a nap,
But since they've bought that canine chap
    You often visit <u>Our</u> House.
That Christmas puppy's constant yap
And disposition for a scrap
Made you prefer the human lap
    Provided here, at <u>Our</u> House.

Your silky black enticing fur
Attracts my fingers like a lure
To smooth your curves and make you purr.
    You savour that at <u>Our</u> House.
It's not for long that you're demur ——
You think of food and start to stir.
Then walking to the fringe, infer
    There're snacks for cats at <u>Our</u> House.

With tail erect and sensing nose
You sniff the herbs beneath the rose,
And start to dig a hole for those
    Events we ban from <u>Our</u> House.
And when once more you want to doze
Audacious cat, you presuppose
The duvet's there for your repose!
    You can't use that at <u>Our</u> House.

So, knowing when your welcome's done
You visit those next-door-but-one,
To find an armchair in the sun.
    A comfy one at <u>Their</u> House.
They offer food you cannot shun,
And, 'though this visit's always fun,
You recognize that, if you run ——
    There's time for number <u>Three</u> House.

And so you have this well planned beat —
You sleep your way along the street!
With people offering lots to eat
    It's like the Ritz at <u>Any</u> House.
You sharpen claws, then stretch your feet.
It's time to quit this final seat
And step back through the flap to greet
    That dog who lives at <u>Your</u> House.

"Maxwell"

Max – the Elegized Cat

When Max was about 130 years old in terms of a human life-span, "it" began to suffer from arthritis. Walking was slow and obviously quite painful, which made Max a target for other cats who wanted to extend their territory. One day I heard it on the other side of the second neighbour's fence, desperately trying to leap onto it. This was something that it hadn't achieved for several months. After a minute or two its front paws managed to grasp the top of the fence, and with a super-feline effort, it managed to drag itself onto the top. Having got there, it furtively looked round. Then it pulled down a stem of the cotoneaster that was growing on our side of the fence, and nibbled the young tip. It repeated this with three other stems, and then jumped back down on the same side of the fence from which it had jumped up. Its' sole objective for all this effort was <u>not</u> to take a short cut to our garden, but to <u>eat tips of cotoneaster</u>! Out of curiosity I tried to discover whether cotoneasters had any known medicinal properties, and found that they contain:-

1. An anodyne similar to acetyl-salicylic acid (i.e. aspirin) that deadens pain.

2. Phenolic glycosides that can have anti-cancer and anti-inflammatory properties.

3. I also discovered that leaves of *alangium salvifolium*, a small deciduous tree or shrub that is found in the hotter regions of India, contain phenolic glycosides, and these leaves are frequently used as a poultice to reduce rheumatic pains.

This begs the question, "How did the cat know what plant might have a beneficial property and not poison it?" Unfortunately Max was taken for a final visit to the Vet just a few days later, so I do not know whether the cotoneaster eased its' condition.

At the time I was suffering with a painful swollen knee that had to be x-rayed and scanned. I was told that it needed key-hole surgery. When I asked whether surgery could guarantee to improve the condition I was told that it might make it better or it might make it worse, and when I asked what would happen if I didn't have surgery I was also told that it might get better on its' own, or it might get worse! I elected to postpone surgery, and try my own remedy. I picked lots of fresh tips from the cotoneaster, put them into the blender, and painted the lurid green staining pulp all round my knee. It felt cool and soothing, like cucumber skin placed on the forehead to reduce a headache, and it certainly had anodyne properties because it numbed the pain. I can not confirm its anti-inflammatory properties because my knee may have got better with rest, but I was back playing tennis just four weeks later.

"Max – the Elegized Cat"

(This is my Elegy to Max, who might have made a novel medical discovery.)

Of cats and cars you had no fear.
You lost a rib and bits of ear,
But stayed "Top Cat"; you had no peer —
      They dare not visit <u>Our</u> House.
Arthritis struck your final year.
You weakened, and it did appear
The end of life was drawing near,
      But still you limped to <u>Our</u> House.

Cats have nine lives in feline lore,
But you dear Max had lives galore —
The Vet was adding up your score!
      You'd often visit <u>His</u> House.
So now, poor Max, you are no more.
There's no meowing at our door.
We've surplus milk! The Vet is poor!
      Your final stop was <u>His</u> House.

On starry nights I stand and stare
At all the constellations there.
I see "The Plough", I see "The Bear",
      But shining over <u>Our</u> House —
A new formation like a Chair,
And on its seat I see a pair
Of amber eyes that seem to glare
      With longing down at <u>Our</u> House.

Your new Celestial home on high
Is that "Great Armchair" in the sky.
You've found the Milky Way close by
      So now you don't need <u>Any</u> House.
But here below we heave a sigh.
We all thought you were quite a guy
And sometimes, still, we wipe an eye.
      We miss you here at <u>Our</u> House.

The Credit Crash

Maybe I'm old fashioned or just envious, but I don't believe that any one is worthy enough to receive a multi-million pound bonus when they already have an income in excess of £1M per year. They should be kept on their toes by the threat of dismissal if they under-achieve. However, if I was earning several millions of pounds per year I would probably think differently, and feel that I deserved a large bonus. The international banking profession receives a total of several billion pounds per year in bonuses, and I am sure many other professions are equally well rewarded. Just think what the buying power would be if all bonuses were put into a communal pot for one year! One could have disaster-relief aircraft containing mobile hospitals, tents, water-purification plants, digging equipment, etc., on permanent standby in every continent. One could irrigate vast areas of desert. One could initiate a program for a voyage to Mars. One could build a computer that not only held every bit of information that man has acquired, but could process it and learn. One could also use it to enable me to have my dream home in every beautiful place in the world, and a jet or luxury yacht to travel between them. Life is very unfair!

The Credit Crash

```
| u - | u - | u - | u - |
| u - | u - | u - | u - |
| u - | u - | u - | u - |
| u - | u - | u - | u - |
```

"Don't leave your cash beneath the bed,
But use a Bank," is what they said,
"And pension funds will all be safe
In Stocks and Shares … if you have faith."

But now I fear for what I own,
And nowhere can I find a loan.
Those Bankers, caring not a toss,
Take bonuses despite their loss.

And what has happened to my shares,
With Brokers playing Bulls and Bears?
My brolly for *that* rainy day
Is inside out and blown away.

But, sitting here with all my woes,
I ought to spare a thought for those
Who've never even had a bed,
Let alone some cash to shed!

I wish that Bankers felt the same
When putting in their bonus claim.
Their attitude makes me despair,
And feel they have no sense of care.

If only I had wealth like them!
I'd mix with other wealthy men
And purchase anything I see,
Ignoring silly prats like me.

Knocking On

Getting old is a strange event. You grow shorter and yet your feet seem to be further away. Your memory of the events that took place many decades ago remain fresh in your mind and yet you forget what you have just started to do. You can't remember the names of friends and relatives, and get very irritable over quite trivial things. You cease to be with the times and still wear a knotted handkerchief over your bald head on sunny days, instead of a sun hat. Buying new clothes seems to be a waste of time because you will never get full value from them. Your ability and concentration reaches rock bottom, so when you try to mend your existing clothes you make them look worse than before the repairs. Bearing all of this in mind, you sometimes forget your age and start flirting like a teenager. Growing old really is strange.

The author aged 70.

The author as he may appear if he is still here in 10 years time.

Knocking On

```
| u - | u - | u - | u - |
| u - | u - | u - | u - |
```

Although I'm losing all my hair,
I'm eighty five, so I don't care.

I'll knot a handkerchief to wear,
I'm eighty five, so I don't care.

I use false teeth, but don't despair.
I'm eighty five, so I don't care.

I place things down, I know not where.
I'm eighty five, so I don't care.

I dress in shorts that have a tear.
I'm eighty five, so I don't care.

And if the shoppers stop to stare,
I'm eighty five, so I don't care.

I've just moved house to Santander.
I'm eighty five, so I don't care.

And found a beach where girls are bare.
I'm eighty five, so they don't care.

I'll sometimes paddle for a dare.
I'm eighty five, so who's to care.

But now I've got this blonde *au pair*,
I'm eighty five, and that's not fair!

Ogof Agen Allwedd

(Llangattock escarpment, Brecon Beacons National Park)

This poem is a little less frivolous than some of my 'Caving' poems. It was written after I began to suffer with a bad back and realized that I would probably never be able to go into 'Aggy' again. I certainly wouldn't reach the Summertime Series. There used to be some inflated floats for crossing the Turkey Pool. One had to sit astride these floats and use the cave wall to push ones' way along. At the end of the short passage, where there was only one wall within reach, it became very difficult to stay upright. We observed, statistically, that the 6th person turned-turtle.

The Main Passage on the way to the Cliffs of Dover was covered by clay that had dried out and shrunk into slabs. A form of gypsum, known as 'selenite' grew up from the clay. Some of the crystals were over 9 inches high. Over the years most of the crystals have been crushed or stolen, and the cracked clay has been transformed into a sandy footpath.

The Cliffs of Dover are about 20 foot high and consist of alternate layers of sand and clay 2 or 3 inches thick. These layers are like the 'varves' discovered in melt-water lakes by the Swedish geologist Van de Geer. They are similar to the growth rings of trees…the coarse layer being deposited when there was turbulent water during the summer, and the fine layer being deposited from the still water when the surface was frozen. Thinner layers within the main bands may represent severe events during a season. The black band is curious. It does not contain any carbon and is very fine. When heated in a reducing flame it formed a lump of almost pure iron.

81

The Myndd Llangattock's northern edge

The 'key-hole' entrance of Ogof Agen Allwedd (Cleft of a key cave)

Ogof Agen Allwedd

The Mynydd Llangattock's northern edge
Is steep, and on it is a ledge;
   The scar from quarrying lime.
Beneath that massive limestone face,
A labyrinth of empty space;
   The handiwork of Time.

The key-hole that unlocks the maze,
Would hardly catch the fleeting gaze
   Of those who do not know
The thrills and beauty held in store,
For cavers, when they first explore
   The hidden voids below.

So let me now, in verse and rhyme,
Take you to the Summertime;
   A Series much renowned.
Put on your boots, your hat, your lights,
Together we'll explore the sights
   Of Aggy, underground.

Unlock the gate, hang up the key,
Sign in the book, and follow me
   Along the entrance crawl.
Then through the Tool Shed we will go,
Pressing on until we slow
   Amongst the Boulder Fall.

In Baron's Chamber we will wait,
And let our group accumulate,
   Before the Second Choke.
Then in the Arm-Chair each will sit
A while, and meditate a bit,
   Preparing for a soak.

For if you really want to gloat,
As each one sits astride the float
　　　Look out for number six.
He'll start in blissful ignorance
Of the whimsic' trend of chance
　　　That lands him in a fix.

At last the distant goal is reached
And Hawkin's Horror has been breached
　　　You're in the Summertime.
And now I'll leave you to explore
Two miles of virgin cave, or more.
　　　A moment that's sublime.

Then, after we have climbed back through
The Second Boulder Choke, then you
　　　Can walk for many hours
Along a paved mosaic way
Of laminated sand and clay,
　　　Among the gypsum flowers.

This major passage leads you through
The Music Hall, and then on to
　　　The Cliffs of Dover chines.
And here the timeless stream still carves
A passage through historic varves —
　　　Annals of different climes.

As we return, the focussed gaze
Of dimming lights through sweaty haze
　　　Brings thoughts of food and tea.
But when the entrance comes in sight,
With fresh sweet air and star-lit night
　　　Please spare a thought for me.

For me all this is now a dream.
I'll go no more down Southern Stream,
　　　My caving lamp is sold.
I'll miss the smell of caving mud,
My beating heart's excited thud,
　　　For I am growing old!

1066 and All That

In 1066, a William and a Harold fought a battle for the English throne. William (nicknamed the Conqueror) was a Norman bastard … literally, and Harold was a brother-in-law of Edward the Confessor. Consequently neither was entitled to succeed Edward the Confessor to the English throne. On the basis of heredity the throne should have passed to Edgar, the grandson of Edmund Ironside who had been Edward's half-brother. There is some evidence to indicate that Edward initially wished William (the Conqueror) to succeed him, but subsequently designated his brother-in-law, Harold. Undoubtedly Harold was preferred by the English nobles, and he was crowned at Westminster immediately after Edward was buried on the 6th January 1066.

Harold had a brother named Tostig, who had been exiled and had fallen in with the king of Norway. They invaded the north of England, and Harold had no choice other than to take an army north to defeat these invaders. He defeated Tostig, and the king of Norway quite decisively at Stamford Bridge on the 25th September 1066, killing both. He had been reluctant to travel north because he was aware that William (the Conqueror) was about to invade from France. This Norman invasion did take place on the 29th September with their landing at Hastings. Harold and his army may have had a few days to feast their victory before they received news of the invasion. The distance between Stamford and Hastings is about 250 miles, and therefore Harold and his army would have needed to average about 25 miles a day for about 10 days, in order to reach Hastings and build defences before the battle. It is not surprising that he lost against an army that was considerably superior in numbers. The photo shows the battlefield at Hastings as viewed from king Harold's encampment.

The whole episode is brilliantly displayed in the Bayeux Tapestry (which is actually not a tapestry). On it, beneath the word "Harold", are two armed figures. One is being hacked down, and the other has an arrow in his eye. We cannot say for certain which is intended to be Harold, but it is traditionally the one with the arrow in his eye. The battle was lost when the Normans feigned a retreat, and the undisciplined English soldiers broke ranks to chase them.

After William the Conqueror became king, he gave lands to the nobles who had supported him. In order to protect themselves from counter attacks, the nobles built wooden fortresses on earth mounds known as "Motts". Many of these wooden fortresses subsequently became Norman castles.

View of the battlefield from Senlac Hill.

If Harold really is intended to be the character portrayed with three arrows in his shield and an arrow in his eye, then he appears to have a black moustache and been hit in his right eye.

1066 and All That

```
| u u - | u u - |              a
| u u - | u u - |              a
    | u u - | u u - | u u - |   b
| u u - | u u - |              c
| u u - | u u - |              c
    | u u - | u u - | u u - |   b
```

After **Har**old's large **force**
Had been **fight**ing the **Norse**
    And the **bat**tle at **Stam**ford was **won**
They were **rest**ing at **York**
Eating **mut**ton and **pork**
    When they **heard** what the **Nor**mans had **done**.

For it **seem**ed at a **glance**
That a **Will**iam from **France**
    Was at**tempt**ing to **cap**ture the **crown**.
There was **no** time to **waste**
So they **tra**velled in **haste**
    To the **South** near a **Sus**sex-coast **town**.

They had **moved** with such **speed**
'twas ap**propr**'ate in**deed**
    The word **Haste**-ings by **chance** was its' **name**.
It was **here** they made **camp**
To re**lax** from their **tramp**,
    Which had **left** them ex**haus**ted and **lame**.

And the **place** that they **chose**
Was on **land** that a**rose**
    So the **Nor**mans were **shoot**ing up**hill**.
This lo**ca**tion made **sense**,
Being **great** for de**fence**,
    And the **Brits** were pre**par**ing to **kill**......

87

'till the **Nor**mans be**gan**
A re**ver**sion, and **ran**,
   But the **run**ning was **mere**ly a **ploy**.
When the **Brit**ons gave **chase**
They turned **arse** about **face**,
   Which made **Har**old a **ver**y cross **boy**.

Then he **said** with a **sigh**
I've been **shot** in the **eye**,
   And he **fell** to the **earth** with a **groan**.
So the **bat**tle was **done**
And the **Nor**mans had **won**.
   That's how **Will**iam ab**duct**ed the **throne**.

But his **lead**ers drew **swords**
For they **want**ed re**wards**
   To which **Will**iam a**greed** to con**cede**.
So he **gave** them all **plots**
To build **cast**les on **motts**.
   And he **grant**ed all **else** they might **need**.

If they **tend**ered a **plea**
He would **al**ways **agree**.
   He'd con**sent** if they **asked** for a **thing**.
As he **al**ways said **"Yes."**
It is **just** what you'd **guess**,
   They called **Will**iam the **Con**currer **king**!

The Mole

This poem is probably only of interest to Primary School Teach**ers**, and young Natural**ists**. It was the first poem I wrote, and it was very nearly the last. I was in the penultimate class before taking the 11+ exam, so I was probably 9 or 10 years old. The teacher had enthralled us by reading a chapter from the Wind in the Willows every week. Then she started reading poems by Rudyard Kipling, particularly those from The Jungle Book. We had never been given homework before, but she asked us to try writing a poem for her to read the next week. This poem was my effort, but she never read it to the class. When she saw it she screwed it up, and threw it into the bin. "You couldn't have written this unaided", she said. "We don't like cheats in this class!"

(Written when aged 9 or 10)

When I went out for a country walk
I met some animals that could talk.
I saw a rabbit go down a hole
And then I saw a baby mole.

Then a fox said unto me
"Where did that rabbit go? I didn't see."
I said he went down a rabbit hole,
Close by that little baby mole.

Then a hound dashing up,
Saying, "Where did go that little pup?"
I said he went down a rabbit hole,
Close by that little baby mole.

Then horse and jock came up with a bound,
And the jockey said, "Where gone is my hound?"
I said he went to a rabbit hole,
Close by that little baby mole.

The horse's hoof got stuck in the hole,
So the jockey fell off and he squashed the mole,
But the rabbit escaped from another hole,
A long way off from the flattened mole.

(Perhaps all of my poems should end up in the bin or loo!)

Seduction in South Wales

During my working life I undertook research at the forefront of Physics and Radar (Infra-red Detectors, Infra-red transmitting Glass, MASERS, LASERS, Electron-spin Resonance, X-ray Crystallography, Semi-conductors, Gunn Diodes, Liquid Crystals, Amorphous Switches, DC-electroluminescence, Energy Storage, Microstrip Antennas, and Phased Array Antennas, etc.). During my retirement I have researched various 15th century characters (Sir John Fray, chief baron of the Exchequer; Lord John Wenlock, diplomat, marriage-broker and spy), I have taken up painting (Watercolour, Acrylic, Oil, and Pastel), and I have continued to write poetry (Lewd and Lyrical). However, my degree was in Geology!

For the latter reason this poem has been written from a Geologist's point of view. However, as my knowledge of geology has become somewhat eroded, there is sure to be someone who will notify me of my geological mistakes. The poem may therefore suffer alterations if it ever gets published again! It might also have a different title. I have emphasised the stressed syllables of the metre so that you can compare it with my previous juvenile effort.

My painting of "The Columns" in Ogof Ffynnon Ddu.

Seduction in South Wales

```
| u - | u - | u - | u - |
| u - | u - | u - | u - |
   | u - | u - | u - | u - |
| u - | u - | u - | u - |
| u - | u - | u - | u - |
   | u - | u - | u - | u - |
```

Your **water-birth** was **long** ago,
Three **hundreds million years** or **so**,
    Be**neath** a **shallow temp**'rate **sea**
Where **crin**oids **waved** and **cor**als **grew**,
Where **oo**lites **rolled**, and **no** one **knew**
    What **you** would **one** day **rise** to **be**.

The **crushed** cretacea **year** by **year**
Crea**ted layers tier** by **tier**
    Un**til** the **sea** with**drew** its' **shield**.
E**rosion from** the **near**by **land**
Had **filled** the **rivers full** of **sand**
    So **millstone grit** be**gan** to **build**.

It **built** its **thick** agg**lom**erate
From **quartz**ite **and** cong**lom**erate
    And **squashed** you **in** your **calcite bed**.
As **hills** eroded **day** by **day**,
The **rivers slowed** and **lost** their **way**
    So **swamps** and **brack**ish **deltas spread**.

These **landfill sites** for **gymn**osperms,
For **lycopocts** and **pt(e)ristosperms**
    Per**formed** a **tree**-em**balming roll**.
The **Mes**ozoic **came** and **went**.
It **pressured you**, and **you** were **bent**;
    Your **swampy cap** was **turned** to **coal**.

The **Mes**ozoic's **loss** was **deft**;
There's **just** the **Low**er **Lias left**;
    This **is** its **only legacy**.
The **rocks** were **soft** and **quick**ly **lost**;
Through **being young** they **paid** the **cost**
    Of **boun**cing **with** isostacy.

91

And **now** we **have** the **Pleistocene,**
When **large** ex**tents** of **ice** were **seen**
  That **helped** to **shape** your **out**er **skin.**
The **melting ice** sank **to** your **core**
To **widen cracks** and **fissures more**
  So **cave** formation **could** begin.

The **rain,** with **carbon from** the **air,**
Formed **acid that** in**creased** your **wear.**
    Phreatic **chambers were** dis**solved,**
And **when** the **raging torr**ents **flowed**
Your **Vad**ose **passage could** erode.
  That's **how** your **caves** in **Wales** evolved.

And **as** each **cave** began to **breathe**
The **drying air** forced **drips** to **leave**
  A **range** of **calc**ite **sediments,**
Like **stalactites** and **stalagmites,**
In **ochre hues** and **textured whites;**
  Or **columns, straws,** and **pediments;**

With **cur**tains, **drapes,** and **wed**ding **cakes;**
And **pearls** that **formed** in **rim**-stone **lakes**
  As **raging torr**ents **were** re**duced.**
These **caves,** your **daugh**ters **of the night,**
Are **all** dressed **up** for **our delight.**
  We **vis**it **them** and **get** se**duced!**

Based upon a smaller scene in Bridge Cave (South Wales)

Imprints in the Snow

Wing-prints of a buzzard. The wing impressions terminate in the distance where the buzzard caught a rabbit. Note how the right wing must have been raised to avoid the twiggy branch. Skilful flying!

The rabbit has been caught and the buzzard brings its wings over and in front of its head to gain maximum lift, like someone swimming the butterfly stroke.

Imprints in the Snow

```
| u - | u - | u - | u - | u - | u - |
| u - | u - | u - | u - | u - | u - |
| u - | u - | u - | u - | u - | u - |
| u - | u - | u - | u - | u - | u - |
```

The ground was hard, and then the pond began to freeze,
As winter whistled through the apple orchard trees.
A rusty leaf or two were all that branches bore,
When winter whistled through, and froze them to the core.

As daylight dimmed the bitter wind began to ease,
And winter night dissolved those apple orchard trees.
Then silently, throughout that apple orchard night,
The winter flurried down to paint the orchard white.

It settled on the trees and thickly on the ground
To form a winter cloak that softened winter sound.
The silent night was broken every frozen hour
By distant bells that shook within their muffled tower.

A hoary moon had watched the winter clouds go by
Until they thinned to show a twinkle in the sky,
And then the moon itself, in all its' glory shone.
Those heavy winter clouds had slowly drifted on.

And after dawn the air was bitter, raw, and rude,
When fur and feathers rose to forage for their food.
No camouflage for fur amongst the winter white,
And feathers in the sky had got the fur in sight.

No traction for that fur, when in its' hour of need
It wished to use its' hopping legs to leap away at speed.
The buzzards' ground attack was made so fast and low
It left its' feathered prints upon the orchard snow.

The rabbit never found a blade of grass to eat.
The buzzard lived by gorging blood-hot rabbit meat.
They both had thought the god of nature would provide,
But one had prospered well, the other sadly died.

What if this orchard snow should last the winter through?
Would other rabbits die if dressed in brown like you?
The genes will favour those who venture out at night,
Or like the Arctic Hare, can change their fur to white.

For laws of Nature show the fittest will survive.
It's ideal genes and luck that helps us stay alive,
But Earth is warming up, and Ice may not move down,
So rabbit genes may favour fur that's tawny brown.

The years have hastened by since that eventful day …
The snow has reached the sea, the buzzard's turned to clay.
Although all life must change, I feel I want to cry …
Those apple orchard trees are carbon in the sky!

———————

When the apple orchard trees were burned they were replaced by more trees, thereby locally stabilizing the environment. However, it appears that the global environment may be becoming unstable.

Most countries throughout the world have at last realized that "Global Warming" is a potential disaster, but I don't believe that the issue has been explained to the public in the best way. Scientists have been trying to demonstrate that, although the climatic cycle has dips and peaks, the overall trend indicates a rise in temperature. The occasional cold winters don't make this phenomena appear to be very urgent.

An alternative way to explain the problem is to note that the extinct fern-like plants responsible for absorbing carbon to form the coal measures, and the various crustaceans responsible for absorbing carbon to form the oil shells, were actually absorbing the carbon for **many tens of millions of years**! At the current rate mankind will have undone that process within the next one hundred years. A sobering thought?

Mankind has been living in luxury by drawing upon our "Deposit Account". We have got to learn to live within our "Current Account", and only use solar, wind, geothermal, tidal, or renewable energy for our needs.

———————

Dogma

I have always tended to question the numerous pieces of dogma that I am expected to believe, no matter whether it involves Religion, Politics, History, or Science. I suppose it started when I questioned how Father Christmas squeezed down the chimney with my Christmas presents. I was told that he got his elves and goblins to do it for him. When I asked how an extra large parcel came down the chimney I was told that this one had been left outside the front door. I then pointed out that none of my other presents were coated with soot! Eventually, when I could do a little mathematics, I realised that it would be absolutely impossible to visit every household during Christmas Eve, and with a little more mathematics I was able to show that Father Christmas would have needed to travel faster than the speed of light. This meant the mass of my presents would have become infinite, and the Earth would have collapsed into them.

None of us can be experts in every subject, and therefore we tend to accept what we are told by the officials or leaders in the various fields, such as Religion, Politics, History and Science. I have observed that many of these "Leaders" have achieved their status by absorbing the dogma that they are taught without really questioning or comprehending various implications in the light of current knowledge. Very often they become despots, or interpret the acquired dogma to suit their personal desires, expecting everyone to accept their interpretations without question. Let us consider a few examples within each of these topics.

It took many generations before any religion would accept that the Earth is a spheroid and not flat, and when leaders eventually modified their dogmas to accommodate this observation, they insisted that this spherical Earth must be at the centre of the universe. In those days anyone daring to suggest that the Earth rotated around the Sun could be burned as a heretic. Members of the Catholic Church persecuted other sects of Christianity, such as the Cathars, in addition to supporting wars against the Muslims. The Cathars had many beliefs that differed from the Catholics, and they did not accept or make payments to the Pope. In particular they did not believe in "Transubstantiation". This is the process whereby bread and wine at the Eucharist are believed to turn into the body and blood of Christ. At the instigation of the Pope hundreds of Cathars were burned alive by the Catholics, just as the Romans had burned and persecuted the early Christians. The Jews, and different sects of the Muslim faith are no better. Al Qaida and Taliban bombers, for instance, have murdered women, children, and fellow Muslims. As Christians, Jews and Muslims believe in a Heaven and a Hell, did those who performed these atrocities ever considered where they will be sent?

Some sects still retain a believe that the Earth was created in 7 days about 4000 years ago, yet we know that Palaeolithic men were hunting animals with stone tools several thousands of years earlier. If these Palaeolithic hunters had a "Religion" it was probably based upon rituals to ensure their hunting success or to appease the animals they hunted, and may account for some of their cave paintings and beautiful carvings. During the Neolithic period, when hunters were becoming farmers, they realised that their crops were controlled by the seasons and began to worship the Sun and Moon. Springs, streams, and rivers, were also regarded as holy. These beliefs developed independently in different Continents, including South America. The Greeks and Romans tended to humanize their gods, and many of these gods were assumed to live in the clouds on top of mountains. The development of Monotheism probably derived from a fusion of these Western beliefs and religious ideas from India and the Far East.

All 21st century religions will have to adapt their dogmas to accommodate Darwin's Theory of Evolution, the Geological age of the Earth, and an appreciation that there is almost certainly life on planets orbiting other suns in this Galaxy or other Galaxies within the Universe. If there are other intelligent life-forms they may not look like us. They could have evolved with more than two arms and legs. They could even have evolved with wings. If they have a Monotheistic religion they may believe that they were created in the image of their god!

The indoctrination perpetrated by Political leaders is usually easier to see in retrospect. By way of examples we may consider Hitler and the rise of the Nazi Party; Stalin and the rise of Communism; British Imperialism and the introduction of the Slave Trade; and numerous civil wars that have occurred in Britain and almost every other country in the world. The human race is easily led by beautiful oratory or pushed by despots, to accept inappropriate dogmas.

In Historical, Archaeological, and Scientific research, gross arrogance, or the falsification of experimental data can perpetrate dogma that should be questioned. There is a classical case of gross arrogance in Archaeology that I must relate as it concerns "Caves and Palaeolithic Art", a subject I have frequently used for one of my lectures.

By the middle of the latter half of the 19th century a lot of prehistoric artefacts had been found in cave entrances. In addition to the bones of prehistoric animals that are now extinct, there were stone tools, and carvings of these animals. These finds indicated that man must have existed at the same time as the extinct animals. A lot of artefacts were exhibited at the Paris International Exhibition of 1878, and an amateur Spanish archaeologist named Don Marcelino de Sautuola became absolutely fascinated by what he saw. Marcelino lived in Santillana del

Mar, and a few years earlier a cave had been found on a piece of land that he owned on the outskirts of Santillana. He began to excavate the cave and found lots of prehistoric artefacts. One day he had his five-year-old daughter with him, and it was she who noticed the paintings of bison and other animals on the cave roof above him. The paintings had been produced by mixing pigments with animal fat and must have been done before the cave entrance was blocked off. He contacted Vilanova, a Professor of Geology in Madrid, and when he visited the cave he agreed that these paintings could not be anything other than prehistoric. The find received a lot of publicity. Even the King of Spain came to see the paintings, but international archaeologists were not convinced. In 1880 there was an International Congress of Prehistoric Archaeology being held in Lisbon. Marcelino submitted his drawings of the pictures to the Congress, and Vilanova made arrangements for the archaeologists to visit this prehistoric cave named Altamira. The most eminent archaeologists from all over the world were attending the Congress. There was Virchow from Germany, Lubbock from England, Cartailhac from France, Pigorini from Italy, Undset from Norway, Montelius from Sweden, and Ribeiro from Portugal. They viewed Marcelino's drawings at the Congress, but none of them had seen anything like this before so they unanimously agreed that it was a fraud. None of them even went to see the originals for themselves. As Marcelino had been accused of fraud he died a broken man. A few years after his death cave paintings were discovered in the Gironde department of France, but it was too late to apologise to Marcelino!

There have been many fraudulent claims in Science, together with the distortion of results and statistics. Before I discuss scientific dogmas, you might like to read the next poem. It reveals that things haven't changed very much during the last 30,000 years, and it could explain the origin of cave paintings!

Hawk-Eye
(or Nothing's Really New)

This poem is full of anagrams, similes and 'orrible innuendos .... I was in my crossword-solving phase when I wrote it! Also I had just returned from visiting some of the prehistoric caves in France; the UK had not long been in the EEC, which was led by Jacques Santer; and, for the first time, my Club had a Scot on the Committee!

This is not a club member, but I happen to have taken this photo of my nephew just before writing the poem.

Hawk-Eye
(or Nothing's Really New)

```
| u - | u - | u - | u - |
    | u - | u - | u - |
| u - | u - | u - | u - |
    | u - | u - | u - |
```

This enigmatic tale takes place
   In Prehistoric days;
When Man the hunter roamed the plains
   Where deer and bison graze.

Cro-Magnon councillors had fixed
   A convocation date
To gather in the south of France
   And have a big debate.

It was important to discuss
   The disappearing bear,
Why mammoths were retreating north,
   And Man was losing hair!

Some blamed it on climatic change,
   Through artificial fires;
On shooting flints into the air,
   Or using tree-trunk tyres.

The Leaders came from different tribes
   Throughout the known lands,
And some arrived in ones and twos
   While others came in bands.

The Van Dale tribe arrived in force,
   Straight from the Nether Plains,
But Elder R. Doe was alone.
   He came from sunny Spain.

From alpine stock came Fredrich Vice;
   (He was the idle one).
Then Jaspa Gheti from Milan
   And Badger Man the Hun.

The Cockney, with his rhyming slang,
   Was Sidney Andertail,
And "Yak the Da", with son and Ma,
   Arrived from Eber Vale.

The cavern where they held this meet
   Belonged to Jaccques Sans-hair.
The roof-top leaked, the floor was damp,
   The walls were bleak and bare.

To Set Aside the hunting time,
   So they could talk all day,
He fed them all on Brussel's sprouts.
   It was the EaCy way.

One morning when he saw the cave
   He nearly blew his lid.
The walls were caked with mural art
   The little Van Dale's did!

I've waffled over Jacques Sans-hair,
   And almost clean forgot
To mention that my hero is
   A brawny hawk-eyed Scot.

This member of the tribe of Gnu,
   With hair of flaming red,
When questioned what he called himself,
   "Hawk-Eye the Gnu", he said.

He'd lots of hair upon his chest
   And hair below the knees,
But did admit the middle bit
   Was rather prone to freeze.

And so he hung around his waist
   A rabbit, fox, and hare,
With fish like salmon, plaice, and cod;
   Yes, every thing was there!

This canny Scot had got the lot,
    It dangled from his belt,
But most of it was still alive.
    And made its' presence felt.

Although these helped to keep him warm,
    He found there was a catch,
It really could be hard for him
    If they began to scratch.

The elders who were gathered there
    Agreed his dress was nice,
But thought it could be modified,
    And offered this advice.

"Now if your garment won't stay still
    You really ought to <u>kill it</u>,
And slippery fish would better be
    If hanging as a <u>fillet</u>."

"The *kill-it* is a great idea."
    They heard the Scotsman say.
"Hawk-Eye the Gnu will gladly do
    What you suggest today."

He gathered up a host of *kill-its*,
    And had the *kill-its* tanned.
Then stuck them to his waist with tar
    To form a wrap-round band.

The moral of this story is
    There's nothing's really new.
The Scots still wear their <u>tar tanned *kill-its*</u>,
    And say "Hawk-Eye the Gnu."

But that's not all, for there is more
    That I can now declare —
They wear the cod piece underneath,
    So now you know what's there!

Gravity

When scientists want to explain a phenomenon they put forward a "Hypothesis" and then devise experiments to validate it. If these are successful the "Hypothesis" becomes a "Theory". When the "Theory" can be accurately modelled mathematically, it may be described as a "Law". These "Laws" are the dogma perpetrated by scientists, and I used to enjoy challenging them.

One of Briton's greatest scientists was Sir Isaac Newton. He put forward a hypothesis to explain why an apple fell to the ground. He supposed that there is a force of attraction between two bodies that varies as the product of their two masses and inversely as the square of the distance between them. When an apple breaks free from a tree the earth and apple are attracted towards one another, but the earth is so massive relative to the apple that it is only the apple that appears to move. This "Force of Attraction" is called "Gravity".

When I was young (aged 19/20) I tried to model a different hypothesis. Instead of gravity acting from within each mass, I supposed that each mass was subjected to a force or source of energy emanating from infinity (i.e. the periphery, or "bow wave" of "The Big Bang"), and that it was this force that was "pushing" them together. I envisaged something like the microwave noise left over from "The Big Bang", but not necessarily an electromagnetic wave. If it was an electromagnetic wave it would have a wavelength much, much, shorter than the shortest gamma wave, such that it would normally pass through the vast voids within atoms and molecules. I supposed that any particle that had a "mass" was absorbing a little of the "radiation", or reflecting it. (Perhaps it was absorbed energy that empowered that particle to exist, like a mini vortex, or radiation wrapped round on itself to form a 3D interference pattern. Although a vortex does not have isotropic properties, a mass containing many such whirlwinds would absorb or reflect evenly from all directions.) As the "radiation" would appear to be coming from infinity, any neighbouring masses would interact with a little of what the other should have received. This would have the effect of mutually pushing them together, and might be interpreted as the mutual attraction that we call gravity. I mentioned this concept to a number of colleagues, but they all thought I was "potty". A Physics or Mathematics student might find it instructive to try developing the equivalent of Newton's gravitational law using the concept.

Newton went on to suggest that the apple had "Potential Energy" whilst it was attached to the tree, and this became "Kinetic Energy" when it was released to accelerate towards the Earth. There is another Law stating that "Energy cannot be created or destroyed". When the apple hits the ground its' kinetic energy is converted into other forms of energy, such as "Heat", "Light", or "Mechanical" (displacement of soil, elasticity, etc.). A Law developed in the 20th century by Albert Einstein goes one stage further. It states that "Mass can be converted into energy", and is described by his famous equation:-

$$E=MC^2 \quad \text{(where "E"= energy, "M" = mass, and "C"= velocity of light.)}$$

That enables me to pose another problem for the university student. Suppose that there are two masses accelerating towards one another under the influence of their mutual 'gravitational' fields, but they are still one light-hour apart. What would happen if one mass was a huge nuclear bomb that exploded, thereby destroying most of its mass. Would the other mass continue to accelerate for an hour? If so, where is the accelerating force? If the other mass does not continue to accelerate, it would mean that the gravitational force had acted instantaneously at this distance, and information had propagated faster than the speed of light! I found it easier to explain this anomaly by invoking my concept that gravity is due to energy being received from the periphery of space. That concept would allow the remaining mass to continue accelerating until it received radiation that had previously been obscured by the exploded mass. The concept of radiant energy inducing a "gravitational" effect would also unify "Gravity" and Relativity. Unfortunately it is difficult to explain all of the more recently discovered particles!

I can pose another problem for the student. Suppose that we have two identical masses with different "entropies", such as amorphous carbon and diamond. If each is converted into energy using Einstein's equation, what has happened to the energy associated with the entropy difference?

As the mass "M" in Einstein's equation can be modified to include "kinetic mass" in addition to "rest mass", it should be possible to modify the equation to include any states of a mass, such as its temperature. If we remove all these possible states by simply considering an isolated and stationary fundamental particle, the only property that we can equate to mass is the attribute we call "spin". Supposing that we could stop this "spin" would the particle cease to exist? If we suppose that the spin is associated with the hypothetical radiation from the periphery of space, there ought to be regions where that radiation is more or less concentrated. Would that cause the fundamental particle to have a different mass? If so, it might not be necessary to introduce the concept of "dark matter" into cosmology because gravitational anomalies could be explained by a slight increase or decrease in the apparent "masses" of fundamental particles! It would also mean that there could be an error in the estimated mass of the universe!

If a mass became very dense, like a "Black Hole", no mass or radiation can escape from its surface, and the hypothetical "very high frequency" radiation would not penetrate through to the other side. One may therefore speculate that neutrons, protons, and electrons might cease to exist at its centre, as it progressively absorbs more mass and radiation at its surface!

If we could increase the "gravitational" attraction between two bodies they would appear to have increased in mass. Suppose that the student could measure the "gravitational" attraction between two very close gyroscopes. (The effects of turbulence, electrostatic fields, and magnetic field being eliminated by a sheet of copper inserted between them.) Would he (or she) discover that this gravitational attraction is different when the rotation of one gyroscope is reversed? When the two gyroscopes are rotating in the same sense as two connected gear wheels the adjacent parts of the peripheries will be travelling at the same speed, and each will see the other's rest mass. However, if one has its rotational direction reversed, the peripheral masses will be accelerating relative to one another, and they will see the "kinetic" masses as greater than the static masses. Will the attraction between these gyroscopes increase as the sum of the peripheral speeds is increased to very high values?

Cosmology was not my field of science, and there have been significant advances since my student days. I therefore expect these concepts will be quickly dismissed by those with the appropriate expertise. The reason for expounding them was to make you stop for a minute or two to think about the fundamental dogma that you have become accustomed to take for granted. Contemplate whether gravity is a consequence of mass, or whether it is the apparent force we call "Gravity" that gives rise to the apparent quanta of "Mass" we call "Particles". Have we been deluded into looking at them the wrong way round?

My next poem deliberately misinterprets Newton's Second Law of Motion, which states that "A body will remain in a state of rest or of uniform motion (i.e. not accelerating), unless acted upon by a Force".

Gravity

```
|u u - |u u - |u u - |u u - |
|u u - |u u - |u u - |u u - |
|u u - |u u - |u u - |u u - |
|u u - |u u - |u u - |u u - |
```

It was **au**tumn when **app**les were **fall**ing from **trees**
On a **day** that was **sun**ny with **scarce**ly a **breeze**,
That a **Cam**bridge-taught **fell**ow was **watch**ing them **fall**
And was **think**ing what **force** could be **caus**ing it **all**.

"If two **mass**es at**tract**, then it's **obvi**ous", said **he**,
"That the **earth** will stay **put** when the **app**le is **free**.
For the **earth** has a **mass** that's a **trill**ion times **more**
Than the **flesh** of an **app**le, its' **skin**, and its' **core**.

As the **strength** of the **force** is re**lat**ed to **mass**,
If the **earth** dis**app**eared, then the **app**le a**las**,
Would be **left** where it **is**, 'though de**tached** from the **tree**,
As there's **no** force to **move** it, 'though **perfect**ly **free**.

If you **give** it mo**men**tum it **keeps** going **straight**,
But sus**tain**ing the **force** gives a **speed**ing-up **rate**.
These e**qua**tions of **mo**tion are **writ**ten as **Laws**,
And there's **no** one on **earth** who has de**tec**ted the **flaws**.

I'll re**veal** to you **now** the most **harr**owing **tale**
Of a **beau**tiful **lass** and a **ve**ry soused **male**.
These two **stu**dents were **sat** in the **stu**dent-run **bar**,
And the **male** was ob**ser**ving from **some**what a**far**.

As the **fe**male a**rose** he be**gan** to re**act**,
For her **bo**dy was **dark** and de**signed** to at**tract**.
When she **sat** in her **car** to re**turn** to her **place**,
He de**ci**ded to **fol**low and to **make** it a **race**.

To ac**cel**erate **fast** and to **wob**ble off **course**,
Was an **act**ion he **knew** must be **caused** by a **Force**,
But the **force** of at**trac**tion was **not** what he **knew**;
'twas the **gra**vity **me**tered by **Bo**dies in **Blue**.

106

Somme Day

A film sequence that is frequently included when the BBC shows documentaries of the First World War depicts a soldier carrying a wounded comrade back through the trenches. (Photo reproduced by kind permission of the IWM). My brothers and I are quite convinced that this soldier is our father, Reuben Forrest Fray. There is a flowery description of the rescue incident in "How I Filmed the War", by Lieut. Geoffrey Malins, O.B.E. He states that these two brave men went in time and time again to bring back bodies and wounded.

Reuben owned a butcher shop and general stores in the village of Westend, near Southampton. When we first saw the film we thought that the way the wounded soldier was being carried was just how our father used to carry the heavy sides-of-beef into the shop from the delivery van (not a fireman's lift or a piggy-back). We wrote to the Imperial War Museum and obtained a large still photo of the soldier, and compared his face with enlargements from some old family photos. We believe the likeness to be quite convincing. What do you think?

At Farm School
(circa 1911)

Trainee butcher
(circa 1914)

Imperial War Museum
(1916)

Whilst a teenager he had attended the Farm School at Basing, but left to become an apprentice at Gough's butcher shop in Southampton. During that period he slipped on a piece of fat and cut his hand badly, consequently he joined the Pioneer/Labour Corps. Initially he was attached to "The Devonshires", and then to "The Australians". One of his tasks would have been to help bring back the wounded and dead, and dig their graves. When visiting the Devonshires' cemetery in France, it was sobering to realise that my father had probably brought back many of the bodies and dug many of the graves.

I can confirm that he was at the Front during the summer of 1916 from a letter that he wrote to one of our uncles.

6th February 1917

> Dear Len,
>   You must think me a <u>fine</u> brother not to scribble you a line for such a long while. This is the first time I think I have written to you since you joined the others by entering upon married bliss. How proud you must feel to have a dear wife & a home of your own, & I hope & trust you are as happy & contented as it is possible to be. I'm sure I'm looking forward to the time when this strife is all over & I am placed in position to make a home for the best girl in the world. But I suppose that day will come some when if we have patience & f-g---y. I wish it had been possible for me to get leave & been home for your wedding, but it wasn't for the lack of my asking. But I expect you know it is very difficult to get back to dear old England when once one sets foot on French soil. All at home have been expecting me on leave for some while but I'm afraid they will all be disappointed as I understand now that leave is stopped altogether for our Battalion this year. I suppose you still make a great study of the operations out here. To us who are here amongst it troubles but a very little I think. We are all anxious to hear news of home & loved ones & welcome letters from home more than anything else. I'm pleased you have escaped the discomforts of a winter out here in the army. It is wonderful what our human frame can stand when it is put to the test. The comfort of a home will appeal to us far more after the experience of this life on Active Service. You used to think it rather hard going to a prepared camp during the summer months in the territorials, didn't you, but here it is far different.
>   It is rather different having to make one's own bivouac in the dusk of an evening with shells screaming over. But is all right when one gets used to it, although the mud and wet like we have had here during the winter takes a little getting used to you may bet. We have had it rather cold here lately. Snow has been on the ground since the 1st January. It isn't so bad when there is no wind, but when the wind is blowing it is awful. I don't remember seeing horses and men with moustaches having long icicles hanging from them like we see here. I'm sure I shouldn't like to be bothered with a moustache this weather. I often laugh at some of them that have them & so much ice clinging on. When I leave my morning's washing water in the old steel helmet all day it is one solid block of ice by the night, so you see how quickly it freezes. Do you think you could wash out of doors in water with ice swimming about in it? I know I thought I could not have done so until now I have to. We have gradually improved our bivouac or dugout, as we might call it, & now it is quite warm &

comfortable. *The floor is sunk down to about 4ft & and the sides made up to about 5ft 6ins with sand bags, so you can imagine a little what it is like. I have a bedstead that I made myself which is far better than the hard ground. I have done away with our old fireplace which was set in the bank of the dugout & let most of the heat go up the chimney, & put in a stove instead made from an old oil drum & a chimney of old cordite cases socketed together. It is surprising how comfortable it is possible to make one's house with a little trouble. The rats are still very fond of paying us a visit at night, tramping over the roof & some times venturing in amongst us, but if we happen to be awake they have to quickly vacate themselves, or perhaps it would not be so well for them if my boot went up against their head.* **We haven't had very dangerous work to do lately. It was a funny experience to be under rifle fire the first time but I haven't experienced this since last summer & I don't particularly want to do so again. Bullets make such a nasty little 'ping' that you get the feeling that the further away from them you are the better pleased one is.** *You haven't heard anything more about your exemption I suppose? Be wise, mind, milking cows is better after all than this life. I expect Mum finds the cold doesn't she? I often think of her as I know the cold doesn't suit her. I suppose things on the farm are much the same as usual, & still many things or rather jobs, that want doing have to be left undone owing to shortage of labour. I think that I shall have another try at my trade if I get home again safe and sound. After this life I expect that I shall want employment a little more exciting than the quiet routine of our farm life. What do you think of old Fritz's latest policy of sinking every ship on the seas? Just like a fellow having a jolly good lacing by fair means & then turning desperate & using any foul means, isn't it? but he's well in the karki boys grip now about this part. I often see the old 'square heads' come back as prisoners after our boys have been over the top to wake them up, but if you heard the preliminary notice they get in the form of a bombardment you would wonder how they could live under it. An air fight is very interesting to watch; It is wonderful how they dodge around one another. I have seen several 'taubs brought down, one of which in a whole mass of fire. When he pays us a visit he doesn't stay long as a rule, & then at a great height. I suppose he thinks it best over his own lines for his own sake. I suppose you find living a little high now as I see prices has gone up rather, but I suppose your wife doesn't bother you much about household expenses. We find it very difficult to get anything in the eating line here. We can get plenty of cigarettes and tobacco, such as it is, but not so good as English. I am having a pipe now as I'm scribbling this, do you go in for the precious weed much? Well dear old 'bro' I don't think of much more to write now, hoping to hear again from you soon & many thanks for your last letters. Trusting you and Laura & all at home are quite well.*

  Ever your affectionate Bro
   Reub.

109

Somme Day

```
| u - | u - | u - | u - |
  | u - | u - | u - |
| u - | u - | u - | u - |
  | u - | u - | u - |
```

I'm crawling here through No-mans-land,
    With bullets overhead,
And colleagues lying close at hand,
    'though most of them are dead.

I'm dragging back a wounded man,
    I hope he will survive.
I'll then return for other men,
    If I remain alive.

I hear a sobbing on my left.
    "Please help!" was all he said.
When I returned to give that help
    The sobbing man was dead.

I prayed that God would let me live,
    The others prayed as well,
But they have found their peace in heaven,
    Whilst I'm on Earth in Hell.

I think I've dug a dozen graves.
    What now must be procured
Are pay-books and the I.D. discs
    Of those to be interred.

The rotting smells of summer's war;
    The bitter cordite taste;
The quagmire of those autumn months,
    And now a frozen waste!

With weather and the human race,
    What more must I withstand?
I'll thank the Lord for Nature's worst,
    And give a helping hand.

Did God create the human form
  To battle and to fight;
Conflicting over crass ideals
  That some believe are right?

What skilful hands or brilliant minds
  Are lost through earthly strife?
What cost afflicts an orphaned child?
  What cost a grieving wife?

We have the brains to contemplate
  Which Dogma should be right,
But as our brains are not the same
  Mankind will always fight.

The men who went 'over the top' were expected to move in an orderly manner towards the enemy, rather like the Pikemen of a previous generation. Those who went out to recover the wounded and dead did have the option of crawling, and that is probably why my father survived.

My father never spoke about the War except to rebuke me one time, and to say that I was lucky to be here. Apparently he was returning to camp after undertaking some repairs on the Albert-Bapaume road when he saw a herd of wild horses about to stray towards the enemy lines. Being a farmer's son he stopped to drive them back in the other direction. While he was doing this a shell landed exactly where he would have been had he continued!

Our existence and our destiny is either a matter of chance, or the will of God, depending upon your beliefs. What appear to be quite trivial events can have a major effect upon the future. A child may be distracted by a dragonfly hovering over a stream or lake. The child could fall in and drown, whereby many tens or hundreds of potential descendants will never come into existence. Alternatively, seeing the dragonfly may encourage the child to become an eminent biologist and make significant discoveries. If my father hadn't cut his hand he might have been one of those who "went over the top", and if he hadn't been a farmer's son he might not have stopped to drive the wild horses away from the Front. In either case, I would not have been born and you would not be reading this Potty Loo Book!

Potting On

During the 2nd World War my father was in the Civil Defence, and I had one brother in Coastal Command and another in the Merchant Navy.

The author aged 4.

Fortunately we all survived. After Peace was declared my father employed two German PoW's to work in the garden and in the 100ft greenhouse where he grew tomatoes to sale in the grocer shop. One day he brought out a spring-board, pommel-horse, and coconut matting from one of the sheds, and set them up so that the Germans could have some exercise and fun during their lunch break. Bearing in mind the number of his friends who had been killed during the 1st WW, and that half of Southampton had been obliterated during the 2nd WW, including the church where he was married. I find it astonishing that he could have shown such compassion.

A lot of large houses and estates had to be sold after the 2nd World War, and my father liked to attend the sales of their contents. As a consequence we ended up with a snooker table in the large upstairs living-room over the shops. I learnt to play and could even do trick shots such as striking down on the cue ball when against the "cush" to make it hit another ball against the "cush" which was snookered by an intervening ball. At 16 I even won 60 cigarettes in a small tournament, but I haven't smoked or played snooker since!

I expect that most readers know the story about a young couple who were in the process of buying their first new house! The house was almost completed, and they were walking around it with the builder to choose their colour schemes. Some of their choice of colours was quite outrageous. In the dinning room, for instance, they decided to have plum-coloured walls with pale green for the ceiling. The builder noted this down in his book and then opened a window and shouted "Green-side up". "Curious!" they thought, as they passed into the kitchen. It was here that they decided the light oak cupboards and fittings would look nice if the walls and ceiling were both painted apple-green. The builder wrote this in his book and proceeded to open the kitchen window and shout "Green-side up". "Even more curious", they thought. Next to the kitchen there was a small downstairs toilet, and all three of them only just managed to squeeze in to it. All of the appliances were white, and they could hardly introduce a contrasting colour right next to the kitchen, so they decided to make it easy for the painters and have that apple-green as well. The builder was only just able to open the little ventilation window and shout "Green-side up". The young man simply could not control his curiosity any longer. "Why is it that you open a window and shout 'Green-side up' whenever we tell you our colour scheme?", he said. "Oh", replied the builder "That has got nothing to do with your colour scheme. Tonight, four of my Irish navvies are going to help set up the snooker tables for 'Pot Black'"

Hidden within the next poem are the names, nicknames, or partial nicknames of most of the famous snooker players, passed and present. How many can you identify? I've forgotten, but I think I included more than 60.

113

Potting On

| u – u | u – u | u – u | u – u |

Although I'm too old to go climbing and caving
I like to keep fit, so I still have a craving
To take up a sport that will make me stay active,
And something to help me keep slim and attractive.
I noticed when watching "Pot Black" on the telly
Some players had cultured a pot on their belly,
But others were tall and exceedingly lanky,
And dressed in apparel that made them look swanky.

I hoped that this sport would fulfil my complacence,
But thought that at times it might test my impatience,
As some of the rules are remarkably testing.
'Though one player plays while the other is resting,
That player may have a long break that's intended,
Yet often takes rests 'though the break hasn't ended!
Then during these breaks they are sometime seen screwing
Extensions that help them reach balls when they're cueing.
They screw their extensions into their cue sockets
Then lie on the baize pushing balls in their pockets.

The ones who are resting are often caught drinking,
Whilst those who are playing chalk tips when they're thinking.
They walk round the table to plan what they're doing,
Then chalk up again before they start cueing.
Arachnids may sometimes be placed on the table!
If balls get too close it would seem these enable
The player escape from the mess he has <u>got</u> in'
So he can continue his session of <u>pott</u>in'.

I wanted to play, so I made the decision
To go to a coach, and to ask for tuition.
He told me to come to his video classes
Of Interesting games with some Up-side-down Glasses.
He said I could learn to pot balls into pockets,
By watching the Spacemen in Starships and Rockets.
And nature was full of remarkable creatures
That offered the game some exceptional features.
The Hawk and the Parrot, the Robin and Eagle,
The Fox and the Shark, the Merlin and Beagle,

114

Had tricks I should learn if I want to be clever,
But playing at speed needs a knowledge of weather.
"Tornados and Whirlwinds, destroy with rotation
The Hurrican's Force causes straight devastation.
The tropical rain from Thai-phoons, in a trice can
Cause flooding; and Blizzards may turn you to Ice, Man.
Welsh Drag on their Macs on a Day when they Wonder
If Gray in the clouds threatens Lightning and Thunder."
The Coach mentioned names that seemed strange and quite silly,
Like Scoobie, and Robbo, and Swampy, and Willie,
And told us some stories of murder and fiction.
His Dracula tales were described with conviction,
And how we should Cope with Magicians and Wizards,
Assassins and Hitmen with Scarface or vizard.
The Outlaw who Pinches from Kings and from Sultans,
With Irish disguise of black Busby and Tartans.
This Fearless Destroyer with Pistol, named Eddie,
Stole Spices and Cream from the Royals, and said he
Would share it with others and not be a Rotter.
And so he formed Bonds with the Carter, the Potter,
The Gentleman's Butler (turned out to Perfection),
And Kids in the street, who had made a collection
To pay off the Bill on a scheme to enable
Them start a new game with an ovoid-shape table,
That makes the best players end up in some tangles
When balls get rebounded at very strange Angles.

While thinking that Snooker seemed Potty and Screwy,
I sat on the Couch with some Noodles and Fuey.
I picked up my chop-sticks and turned on the Telly.
Then, seeing some soccer thought "This has more welly!
It's faster to play and it's easy to figure;
There's only one ball and the pockets are bigger."
That football's a game for old age, you can't quibble;
I'm seventy two and I'm learning to dribble.

I am probably one of the few men who have never played in a football match.
The college that I attended played rugby during the winter months and it was a
taboo to play football. I would have been put in Detention for dribbling with a
tennis ball!

115

To Doreen

I am finishing this booklet with poems written to my first wife, Doreen, and to my second wife Jean, to both of whom this book is dedicated.

This is a photo of Doreen taken about 5 years after we were married. The first poem was written just before we got engaged, and when I was writing 'romantic' verses.

This photo of us was taken in 1988, just a year before she died. The second poem was written when I was sad, depressed, and angry, after her death.

To Doreen

```
| u - | u - | u - | u - |
    | - u - | u - | u - |
        | - u - | u - |
| u - | u - | u - | u - |
    | - u - | u - | u - |
        | - u - | u - |
```

A hundred trillion stars by night
  Cannot give one tenth the light
    Of the sun by day;
So with ten thousand words or less,
  How can fools like me express
    All we want to say?

I wish that I could synthesize,
  Congregate and rationalize
    All my thoughts to one.
I wish Apollo, god of light,
  Could replace my verbal night,
    By a blazing sun.

For there's no single word I know
  That could ever hope to show
    What you mean to me.
Regardless of how well I try,
  I could search my verbal sky,
    For eternity.

Yet as the moon attracts my gaze,
  So I think there is a phrase
    That reflects the light.
Alas it still is but a gleam,
  Just a sallow mirrored beam
    From a satellite.

And like the moon this phrase is old,
  Modest words so often told,
    I will use them too.
This simple plagiaristic way
  Expresses what I want to say,
    "Darling, I – LOVE – YOU."

In Memoriam

u -	u -	u -	u -	u -
u -	u -	u -
u -	u -	u -	u -	u -
u -	u -	u -

When told that you had cancer of the breast,
    You didn't pule or cry,
But bravely faced the certain fact of life,
    That everyone must die.

You knew that death was only weeks away,
    But smiled at me and said,
"Don't do things so because I'd want them so,
    But your way, when I'm dead."

I gripped your hand throughout that fateful night,
    Then held you to my chest
Until you breathed that final piercing gasp
    Before eternal rest.

I sometimes hold your lock of golden hair,
    And loose a gentle sigh,
Or gaze upon your ever smiling face
    And dream of days gone by.

Those happy days, which gleam like moistened pearls
    Upon the sands of time.
Sweet memories which I thought we'd always share,
    Must now be only mine.

I know full well that nothing can withstand
    The unrelenting sea;
I just regret that when the covering tide returns
    Those memories die with me.

It was your dying wish that I should not
    Be doleful or forlorn
And waste my life in sedentary gloom,
    But seek a second dawn.

And so I'll try to live a second life
    With memories that are new,
But at the ending of each fruitful day
    I'll always think of you.

To Jean

After Doreen died I travelled a lot, camping in Alaska, visiting the Galapagos Islands, and undertaking an Everest trek. I have snorkelled off coral beaches in Malaysia, with sea lions, turtles, and penguins in the Galapagos, and dolphins in the Red Sea. During my travels I met Sir Edmund Hillary and nearly tripped up George Bush, Senior, in Abu Dhabi. Then I met and married Jean.

Together we have continued to do a lot of travelling, abroad and in the UK.

Our little camping van has made NEWS. In it we drove to Dunnet Head, the most Northerly point in the UK mainland; to the most Easterly point near Lowestoft; to the most Westerly point at Ardnamurchan; and to the most Southerly point at the Lizard. A far more interesting journey than that from John O'Groats to Lands End! We hope to undertake a revised version one year, and make NEWS independently in Wales, Scotland, Ireland and England.

Together we will drive or sail into the sunset, endeavouring not to waste a minute of our lives, and we will leave the world to our children and our grandchildren.

My final poem is to her, for the support she has given me.

To Jean

| u - | u - | u - | u - | u - | u - | u - |

When walking passed my garden fence you stopped to say hello
While I was staking runner beans, and weeding with a hoe.
The clothes I wore were torn to shreds, and that embarrassed me,
For you were in your Sunday best, and walking down to see
A bride who was about to leave on this her wedding day.
I could not follow dressed like this, but saw her drive away
By standing near the garden fence, and looking down the street.
When you returned we spoke again, to make a date to meet.
As you and I were on our own and on the same estate,
It seemed to be a nat'ral thing that we should start to date.
We started going out for walks, and had a lot to say.
When both of us were home from work we'd meet up every day,
And as our likes were much the same, it seemed a natural thing
That we would tour the jew'lry shops to find a wedding ring.

We've been together eighteen years, and travelled far and near.
We've been to lands where they are poor, or where they live in fear.
We've seen volcanoes, mountains, jungles, ice and sands,
The riches and the poverty in many far off lands.
Whilst in this pleasant land of ours we've seen its' far-flung views....
By travelling to its furthest points ... our camping van made NEWS.
We think of things we have achieved; events we have enjoyed,
And hide away the sad events and things that have annoyed.
So in this world we've lived and loved, and lived to love again.
Our minds are free, our mouths not gagged, our bodies bear no chain.
We are not rich, we are not poor, we're barely middle class,
And as we do not seek for more, we mingle with the mass.
Yet in this world we've been, and seen, and done so many things,
Despite the loss of those who're dear, and problems Nature brings.
The clock of life is wound at birth, and quickly ticks away.
In time we know the spring will go, so treasure every day.

Don't let your life be just a dream, you shouldn't sit and rue
But strive to get the best from life, and make some dreams come true.

A Concluding Statement

This *"-ists, -ers and -ians Potty Loo Book"* has included crude poems, humorous poems, sophisticated poems, jokes, profound statements and some controversial ideas. Although you may disapprove of some items and dispute others, bear in mind that I have tried to provide something amusing and thought-provoking for all tastes. The interpretation of data by Scientists, Historians, Religious Leaders, and Politicians can be erroneous, subjective, biased, and bigoted. What appears to be an obvious or flawless argument may prove to be incorrect. When I used to give talks about Palaeolithic Art I was frequently asked to give my personal interpretation of Cave Paintings. Did I agree that they really were the work of a Shaman? I usually made the following reply.

"Imagine that the whole of the human race became extinct as the result of a virulent plague, and that several thousands of years later an intelligent life-form arrived in Europe from a distant solar system. During the course of their excavations they notice that each village, town and city contains one or more large buildings surrounded by the bodies of numerous members of the human species. Curiously, nearly every one of these buildings contains a statue, engraving, or painting of a young female holding a child. Also, nearly every one of these buildings contains a statue, engraving, or painting of a young male nailed to a cross. The interpretation is perfectly clear. The population had obviously been increasing at an alarming rate. Packing people into urban accommodation to allow more space for growing food was clearly insufficient, and therefore a male was crucified once he had sired a child (probably a slab at the east end was used for this purpose), and the female was only allowed to rear that single child. This civilization was obviously quite primitive because it didn't understand methods of contraception or abortion."

The invading life-form would probably conclude that this was the most probable explanation. How else could they interpret the data? It is highly unlikely that they would ever learn the real interpretation.

I agreed that some of the cave paintings may have been the work of a Shaman, and those may have a religious significance, but others could be teaching aids, forms of communication, records of specific events, or simply art for art's sake. We may never know for certain. Bear in mind that that the various examples of Prehistoric Art range over a period of about 30,000 years! During that timescale

121

there could have been numerous Prehistoric Geniuses, and numerous changes in thoughts and beliefs that could have influenced carvings and paintings.

I hope that this booklet has amused you, stopped you being hoodwinked by dogma, encouraged you to keep an open mind, and made you realize that you should try to end each day feeling that you have achieved something, even if it only involves making someone smile. Remember that your simplest action may be "the butterfly" that triggers some important event several generations into the future!

Acknowledgements

The two lead-in photographs are the copyright of Churcher's College, and the Institute of Electrical Engineers, respectively.

The photograph of the OXFAM Loos on page 13 is naturally the copyright of OXFAM (please support it).

My sketches between pages 24 and 30, of various items connected with Palaeolithic Art, are based on illustrations in several different books on the topic. The original artists are no longer living!

The photo of a small section of the Bayeux Tapestry on page 86 is reproduced by verbal permission of the Exhibition Centre. (The English "audio guide" is excellent, and worth every Euro of the hire fee.)

The photo from the film sequence by Lieut. Geoffrey Malins, O.B.E., is reproduced by kind permission of the Imperial War Museum.

Finally, I would like to thank my wife Jean for her help and support, and her painting on page 42.

p.s. I almost forgot to thank Dick Lexit, my schizophrenic computer, for chequeing my spelllings and Grandma.